The Subject of Adolescence:
Applying Biblical Principles To Your Daily Life

~ A Parent & Me Devotional ~

Tenisha N. Collins

SCRIPTURE QUOTATION COPYRIGHTS

These permission lines were found at:

http://www.biblegateway.com/versions

Scripture quotations marked (MSG) are taken from the Message Bible, Copyright © 1993, 1994, 1995, 1996, 2000, 2001, 2002. Used by permission of NavPress Publishing Group. (MSG)

Scripture quotations marked (NIV) are taken from THE HOLY BIBLE, NEW INTERNATIONAL VERSION, NIV Copyright © 1973, 1978, 1984, 2011, by Biblica, Inc. Used by permission. All rights reserved worldwide.

Scripture quotations marked (NKJV) are taken from the New King James Version. Copyright © 1982 by Thomas Nelson. Used by permission. All rights reserved (NKJV)

Scripture quotations marked (NLT) are taken from the Holy Bible, New Living Translation, Copyright © 1996, 2004, 2007 by Tyndale House Foundation. Used by permission of Tyndale House Publishers, Inc., Carol Stream, Illinois 60188. All rights reserved.

Scripture quotations marked (ESV) are taken from the ESV Bible (The Holy Bible, English Standard Version). ESV Permanent Text Edition (2016). Copyright © 2001 by Crossway, a publishing ministry of Good News Publishers. The ESV text has been reproduced in cooperation with and by permission of Good News Publishers. Unauthorized reproduction of this publication is prohibited. All rights reserved.

The Cure for Adolescents: Applying Biblical Principles To Your Daily Life

ISBN-13: 978-1986291101

ISBN-10: 1986291103

Copyright © 2018 by Tenisha N. Collins

Cover Design by Ginaona, Fiverr.com

Printed in the United States of America. All rights reserved under International Copyright Law. Contents and/or cover may not be reproduced in whole or in part, in any form or by any means, without the express consent of the author and/or Publisher.

Table of Contents

Foreword..5

Family Foreword..6

Dedication..7

Purpose of Devotion..8

How To Use This Book 9

Day 1: Positive Confession..11

Day 2: Being A Good Friend......................................14

Day 3: What If I'm Not Pure?....................................17

Day 4: Your Soul..20

Day 5: Sex, Purity & Dating.......................................23

Day 6: Sex, Purity & Dating, Part II: The Benefits of Abstinence..........26

Day 7: Being Honest..29

Day 8: What To Do When Things Don't Go Your Way..............................32

Day 9: Fighting The Good Fight................................35

Day 10: Politics and Christianity...............................38

Day 11: I Like Me...41

Day 12: What Do You Want? (Coveting)..................44

Day 13: Peaceably Agree To Disagree......................47

Day 14: Who Are You Hanging With?.......................50

Day 15: What Are You Saying?..................................53

Day 16: What Are You Listening To?........................56

TABLE OF CONTENTS

Day 17: Your Thoughts Become Your Behavior..................................59

Day 18: You ARE Valuable..62

Day 19: How To Make Friends..65

Day 20: Refuse To Care About What Others Think..........................67

Day 21: Don't Worry, Be Happy..69

Day 22: Obeying Your Parents..72

Day 23: Who You Represent?..75

Day 24: PMS (Controlling Your Emotions).......................................78

Day 25: Social Media..81

Day 26: The Good Employee...84

Day 27: Church & Bible Study..87

Day 28: Family Over Everything..90

Day 29: How Can I Talk To God If I'm living In Sin?......................94

Day 30: God & The College Life...97

Day 31: Chores & Your Reasonable Service....................................100

Salvation...103

About The Author...104

FOREWORD

"Mom, what's a flip phone? Where is my fidget spinner? Bye Felecia! Make-up on fleek! Wait! "On Fleek" recently graduated to "Snatched!" These are just a few of the interesting phrases or questions you may encounter from "Generation Y" (i.e. Millennials) in the 21st century! It's a different world from where we come from and with so many different challenges!

In this heartfelt devotional, *The Cure for Adolescence: Applying Biblical Principles To Your Daily Life*, "Generation X" new author, and my great longtime friend, Tenisha Collins, gives strategies and guidance to help "Generation Y" adolescents conquer many of the challenges they face in this century on a daily basis.

Smart phones and social media have exploded over the last 10 years providing this generation with so many voices vying for their attention. Now more than ever, those voices of fear, doubt, low self-esteem, depression, and anxiety do everything in their power to usurp authority over and distract them from the voice of God and His plan He has laid out for them in His Word (The Bible).

Tenisha confronts these destructive voices head on! From being a good friend, to being a great employee; from abstaining from sex before marriage, to fighting the good fight of Faith, she pours her heart into each devotion, while using personal life experiences to provide answers and strategies to overcome every obstacle. You will find incorporated at the end of each devotion, scriptures to study (meditate on), a prayer, and confessions (declarations) to repeat, that help YOU put God first, making Him a priority in life.

I believe this devotional is a win-win for parents and adolescents to read and ingest together as they search for and find answers to many natural and spiritual challenges in life! If you read, listen to, and apply these principles laid out in this devotion, your crooked paths will be made straight! You don't have to re-invent the wheel – just follow her lead! Tenisha has written out the plan and made it plain so that you can avoid rough roads along the way. Happy reading and enjoy the journey!

First Lady Minister Carmen D. Byars

Fountain of Faith Christian Center

Louisville, KY

FAMILY FOREWORD

Growing up is hard, especially while in high school where things are constantly changing. With this devotional, kids will have a guide to help them go, and grow, through life. Faith plays a role in my life; it always provides me with something to believe in. With my faith in God, I'm able to trust in Him and not worry so much about things. My mom put so much hard work and love into this book and I hope you can relate to it and that it helps improve your life for the better. Thank you for reading this devotional.
-Joy (15)

Kids as well as young adults will learn that no matter what they've gone through, or going through now, God will always accept them for who they are. As long as you reconnect with God, your life will be taken care of. After reading this book, I felt like I had a second chance to be with the Lord. I think YOU will as well. Faith plays a part in my daily life. I know that if I stick to a plan and pray on it, while listening for what God says, there is no possible way I can fail. And if something doesn't go the way I planned, I don't give up, but pray and ask God for the next step I should take. I think this book is going to help you successfully walk through whatever life brings you.
-Chris (24)

Young adults reading this devotional will learn how to ask God for help. They'll be engaged in a deeper understanding of bible verses as well as know how and when to use them in their daily lives. When I read this book the first time, it brought me back to the memories that were attached to the stories shared. It made me wish I knew how to apply God's Word into situations I face, to help me get through it. Faith plays a significant role in my life. After all, it is my name. I pray every day for my family, friends, school, and myself AND I believe what I say. But even though I believe, I like to have my mom add her faith to my prayer to further increase my chances of having them heard. And from what the bible says, He's always right with me. He never sleeps, and He never takes a nap. I am a work in progress but I know I can always count on Him when I'm in need.
-Faith (17)

Young adults and adolescents will learn that we must constantly assess and evaluate the people we choose to have around us. I was naive in high school, as I'm sure a lot of adolescents are, but this book will help. Readers will learn to ignore negative thoughts and surround yourself with likeminded, goal seeking and God-fearing men and women. We can be and do better. This devotional is the first step. Happy reading.
-Daniel (21)

DEDICATION

This devotional is dedicated to the One who loved me first. The Lover of my soul. My Creator, Master, Father, and Savior. I am forever grateful for His love, wisdom, peace, forgiveness, forbearance, safety, victory and prosperity. Because of Him, I can be me; the me He created me to be.

I would also like to thank my cheerleaders: my husband, Chris, and our four children: Chris II, Faith, Daniel, and Joy. My husband is such an inspiration to me. I am proud of all that he has and will accomplish in life, but I am even more appreciative of his love of Christ. Husband, thank you for loving and supporting me like Christ; I love you. My children truly are gifts from God! When the doctor said I could not have children, Doctor God gave me four! I am forever indebted to God for blessing me with the honor of being their mother. Chris II, Daniel, Faith and Joy, you are truly my greatest treasures!

My family is such a blessing to me. They motivate me to continuously strive to be a better ME. I hope that after reading this devotional, they will not only know me more but be moved to love and understand our Father God more. The devotions featured are glimpses of some of the delicate conversations I've had with my children growing up and how my husband and I taught them to deal with, and overcome, life's obstacles using their faith in God. I am so thankful that they trust me enough to allow me to fill this book with the content of our lives.

I must also thank all the individuals who God used to encourage me to get up and fulfill one of my dreams. My mother in law was very instrumental in forming the skeleton of this book. Little does she know how God used her mouth and voice to speak reinvigorating life back into a dream He had given me when the kids were babes. Thank you, Vivian Jean Collins.

My Wife Talk mastermind partners rooted me on and kept me accountable. Thank you, Anitra Jones, Dr. Michelle McCormick, and Susan Wagers Johnson, for encouraging me to keep writing. Thank you, Notoris Robertson, for making sure I was sticking to my schedule. Treshelle Williams, Founder and President of Wife Talk Inc., inspired me to shift my thinking and pressed upon me the importance of doing everything in a spirit of excellence. She shared a leadership course with me, and that is where the flames were again stirred, urging me to write. Thanks, Fearless Leader. #WifeTribe #WifeTalk4Life

A smile pops on my face and joy fills my heart when I think about one of my favorite First Ladies, the author of the foreword of this book: Minister Carmen Byars! She is an amazing woman of God who gave me her time, knowledge and expertise. I am forever grateful for her friendship, her gift of teaching the Word of God and her willingness to help me on this project. Thank you, sister! I love you to life!

To my parents, Raymond and Felecia Johnson: Thanks for believing I can do anything, for always supporting me, and for your unconditional love. Your love for me opened the door for me to receive the Love of God! I love you both!

To all my readers: I appreciate your reading what I have written. I have written it with YOU in mind. It is my heart's desire that YOU are brought to your knees, before our Father, to give Him time, authority and Lordship of your life. I want YOU to understand just how easy it is to develop a habit of making Him *the* priority of your life. You need to realize that He loves YOU and has already provided everything you will ever need or desire. He wants YOU to live a joyful, abundant life of peace in Him. This devotional will help you start that journey. Just give Him your first and best; give Him all of you. He wants YOU in His presence!

PURPOSE

Imagine that you were born for a specific purpose. Your parent had a terminal disease affecting their internal organs. The only way for your parent to survive is to have a biological match donate several of their organs. Your parents decide to create YOU to harvest your organs. Once you were born, and your parents saw your face, they instantly loved you. They loved you so much; they could not go through with the surgery. They chose to die, so you don't have to.

So, it was with Jesus! He CHOSE to die, so WE don't have to AND we DO have a purpose here on earth. Our mission, in general, is to worship the Father. Our reasonable service to the Father for His loving sacrifice —worshipping Him -- is our purpose. Many followers of Jesus WANT to make God their priority, but with the cares of life and their hectic schedules, they either feel as if they don't have the time or that they don't know how to make God their priority.

Making God your priority is a habit that MUST be learned. Developing a routine requires repetition and discipline. It also necessitates a change in your thinking. You must BELIEVE that it is crucial for you to devote yourself to Him and that you have the time to do so. If you're reading this book, you've already decided to dedicate yourself to Him and have chosen the avenue in which you plan to start showing Him your devotion.

Making God your priority consists of many things: devotion, prayer, meditation, confessing the Word, church attendance, tithing, helping the poor, bible study, feeding the hungry, witnessing, clothing the naked, etc. At first glance, it can seem overwhelming. However, it can be as simple as devoting yourself to Him first thing in the morning. Before you check email, browse your social media feed or shower, take the first 15 minutes of your day to get your mind on God. This devotional will assist you in the first steps of growing your relationship with the Father. To keep your mind on Jesus, use this devotional first thing after you wake, the last thing before you fall asleep or both. Just read the passage, glean the lesson, meditate on His Word, pray and make your confession. This habit will propel you into desiring more from the Father and inspire additional ways to spend more time with Him. If you are a parent reading this with your child, you will also create wonderful memories and strengthen your relationship with each other and with God. What better way to teach your child to love the Lord with all their heart, soul, and might than to use this devotional as a tool.

One last note regarding the purpose of this devotional. Every topic discussed in this devotional is meant to go hand in hand with the others. Every issue is intertwined with the other just as the Bible connects all God's principles, commands, and statues. What does that mean? You can be honest, but be a shady friend, or you can be a virgin but be a liar. The purpose is not to garner the lesson and master the principle behind it to the neglect of the other topics discussed. God wants us to learn all His statutes, laws and commands. We can do so when we master love. Love fulfills all requirements. When we walk in love towards all, including ourselves, we have learned the topics covered in this devotional and much more!

How To Use This Book

I've designed this book to make devoting yourself to God SIMPLE. It can be read alone or with a parent, child, friend or church group. Using this book as a tool to help you develop a habit of spending time with God is as simple as following a few steps.

1.) Pick a time to commune with God. Review your schedule to determine when you are most alert. Choose a time in which you can give ALL your attention and energy to God. If you're having problems determining

what the time should be, pray and ask God to reveal the best time for you.
2.) Now that you have a scheduled time, use this devotional as a tool to assist you in developing a habit of spending time with God. Read the passage, glean the lesson, and meditate on the scriptures. Take your time; take notes and reflect. Finally, recite the prayer and say the confession out loud.
3.) Repeat #2 until you complete the book. Spend some time reflecting on what you learned in the last 31 days. You may want to adopt a certain confession to say daily or you may need to go back to certain lessons when you have a particular need.
4.) Read it again! Research shows that new habits are formed by repetition for at least 66 days. Remember to enjoy the process of forming the habit; don't rush it.

Definitions

Words in the English language can have various meanings. To have effective communication, we need to know which definition applies to the words we're using so that we are on the same page.

***Meditate** = to mutter out loud to oneself; deeply think about or ponder; concentrate on a thing for a period; commit to memory; plan mentally; mutter day and night; repeat over and over again; NOT like a yoga exercise.

***Pray** = talking to God just like you talk with a friend; may include singing; a conversation with God; listening to God speak to you; in English or a heavenly language (other tongues, Acts 2:4); pray TO GOD in the name of Jesus.

{Side Note: For prayer to work, it must be done in faith. You MUST believe you receive what you're praying for WHEN you pray. Mark 11:23. Thus, pray the prayer once then continue to thank God until your prayer is a reality. You never have to pray that same prayer again. If you do, it's just like erasing the first prayer and starting all over.}

***Confession** = to say what God says; verbally declaring God's Word; speaking things in line with what the Word says; speaking what you believe or desire to manifest that is consistent with a godly life; NOT like what you do with a Catholic priest or police interrogation.

Day 1: Positive Confession

God instructs us to meditate on His Word day and night, so that we may be careful to do everything written in it (Joshua 1:8). When we do so, we are prosperous and successful in every area of life. The more time we spend meditating – {pondering, thinking deeply about or focusing on a thing for a period; consider; plan mentally} -- the more we will see the benefits in our life. When we know what His word says, we have confidence in it and can fully trust God.

Something is compelling about speaking His word! His word has the power within itself to do whatever it was sent out to do! Check out Isaiah 55:11 and Jeremiah 1:12. Don't fret about not having the energy or ability to stand on His Word, because He has anointed us to stand firm on His Word already! (2 Corinthians 1:21). Besides, whatever we decree in Jesus' name, in faith, it shall be established, because He cannot lie. He promised that His wisdom would shine upon our plans and decisions (Job 22:28).

Every child of The King needs to know HOW to make the right kind of confession. Your confession will control your life, and your level of faith will never rise above your confession. So, it is imperative that you LEARN how to make the right kind of confession to align yourself up with God's Word. The things stored inside you – your heart or soul – will come out of your mouth; it's a spiritual law. How does it get in there? Through the gates of your eyes and ears. That is why it is essential to guard yourself as to what you watch or hear. Faith comes by hearing, no matter if it is positive, harmful, holy or impure.

Did you know that you are the SUM of all you have been believing and saying about yourself ALL your life? Whatever you believe, you will speak. Proverbs 18:21 says that death and life are in YOUR tongue. You can talk yourself into sickness, health, poverty or prosperity; its up to you. If you want to have what the Word says you can have, your mouth and heart must line up with God's Word. Believing with your heart and confessing the same thing with your mouth are the keys to positive confession.

When I was around five months pregnant with my third child, the doctor discovered that my baby had a congenital disability. The disability was terminal so he recommended abortion as a solution. Fortunately, I knew the power of positive confession and declared that my baby was healed. Although the doctor didn't believe me, it did not stop me from confessing that she was healed. After I prayed for her total healing, I praised God for it. I meditated on healing scriptures and declared my baby healed. I read all the accounts of healing in the Bible and continuously spoke what I believed in my heart to be true. I have what I said. My baby was born perfect, just like God designed her to be.

When you speak, what God speaks, you positively confess power over your life! Be mindful of what you're saying about yourself and your situation. Never divulge your doubts and make every effort to keep your routine of praise, prayer, devotion, meditation, positive confession and bible reading. Your habit will usher you into a stronger, closer relationship with the Father and give you great joy.

Notes

Meditate

...for out of the abundance of the heart the mouth speaks.

Matthew 12:34, NKJV

...whosoever shall say unto this mountain, be thou removed and be cast into the sea; and shall not doubt in his heart, but shall believe that those things which he says shall come to pass; he shall have whatsoever he says.

Mark 11:23, NKJV

For as he thinketh in his heart, so is he:

Proverbs 23:7, KJV

Prayer

Father, thank You for creating me in Your image and likeness. I choose to speak what You say, and I elect to believe what You say about me. I trust You, Father. I will not allow doubt or negative circumstances to sway me, for the things that I can see are subject to change. Father, thank You for giving me the option and privilege to harmonize my confession with Yours. I will hide Your Word in my heart so that when I speak, it will glorify You. In Jesus' name, amen.

Confession

I declare that I keep my mind stayed on God, and I rest in His perfect peace. I only speak what God says about me and my situation. I will not express doubt and unbelief because I am not an unstable man. I receive answers from God through prayer. God has already worked out my situation to my advantage. I serve, love and worship a great God who loves me and has the best for me. I think I am His best; therefore, I am and I have what I say.

Day 2: Being A Good Friend

James 2:23 and 4:4 tell us who we should be friends with and who we shouldn't be friends with. It can be hard sometimes, though. Peer pressure or fear of having no friends can lead you to choose unwisely.

My son was extremely popular as a high school freshman because he was a fabulous football player. He had practiced with the high school football team and was selected, as a seventh grader, to join the team. He had a natural talent and was fun to be around; everyone wanted to be his friend.

He welcomed all the attention, especially from the girls, and chose to hang out with all the social groups once he attended high school. Junior and Senior high school students wanted to hang out with this freshman; it was unheard of!

I'm sure it was exhilarating for him to have high school seniors invite him into their inner circle, but he wasn't very selective about who he hung out with. It seemed as if the entire school accepted him as a friend. Unfortunately, he chose to hang with a group of boys that were not on the right path. They drank alcohol, abused prescription drugs and were not virgins.

Show me your friends, and I can determine your character; you BECOME who you hang around. The bible tells us in 1 Corinthians 15:33 that bad company corrupts good character. Hanging around those boys persuaded my son to change his way of thinking (virgins until marriage, no alcohol use, no drug use, etc.). He wasn't a terrific friend either. He knew that their actions would lead them down the wrong path, but rather than be a good friend and lead by example, he imitated them.

My son lost the opportunity to minister to these boys the minute he fell into the same trap as they did. His character was blemished, his witness made void, and his influence lost. He lost the position of leader, lost his excellent reputation and pushed his values to the side.

Being a good friend is important. God grants every one of us a sphere of influence over a specific group of individuals. It is up to US to use that influence to persuade them that #1) God loves them dearly, #2) God desires to walk with them and #3) it's to their advantage to serve Him.

Being a GOOD friend means listening, caring and loving others despite their faults. It means being honest and compassionate without judgment or condemnation. It's sharing, laughing together and helping one another. You love like Christ when you're a good friend.

Your close friends should be full of wisdom, honest and full of the Holy Spirit. Just look at Jesus' inner circle: Peter, James, and John. Yes, they will have faults, but their primary intent is for your good and vice versa.

My son learned a valuable lesson; that's part of life. We don't always make the wisest choice the first time around. Today, he is a good friend; someone who you can count on, trust and talk to. I share his story so that you may learn from his mistakes and be a light in the lives of those you meet.

Notes

Meditate

You adulterous people! Do you not know that friendship with the world is enmity with God? Therefore, whoever wishes to be a friend of the world makes himself an enemy of God.

James 4:4, NKJV

And the scripture was fulfilled that says, "Abraham believed God, and it was accounted to him as righteousness"- and he was called a friend of God.

James 2:23, NKJV

Prayer

Father God, I delight myself in You. You are holy, worthy of all praise and the lover of my very soul. Thank You for listening to me when I pray. For You to hear is for You to answer; thus, I magnify Your name and give thanks for my requests being granted. I ask for good, Christian friends. Friends who will influence me for good and encourage me to act like Jesus. I ask You for guidance in selecting friends, how to be a good friend and how to use the influence You gave me for Your glory and honor. I thank You for calling me Your friend; just as Abraham believed, I believe. I declare that I am not friends with the world system, for I allow my light to shine brightly for all men to see. Thank You for Your love, peace, and wisdom. In Jesus' name, amen.

Confession

I am a friend of God. He loves me unconditionally. I choose my friends wisely for I have the mind of Christ and the wisdom of God. I know how to be a good friend and how to choose my friends carefully because the Greater One lives on the inside of me. I influence those in my company, and I use that influence for good, for the glory of God.

Day 3: What If I'm Not Pure?

When you give your life to Jesus, your body belongs to Him, and it is your reasonable service to please Him with your body. Since your life, and body, belong to God, that means that every area of your life needs to be yielded to His Lordship. That includes your sexuality. Purity – keeping all sexual thoughts and actions strictly between a husband and his wife – is always THE guideline and priority.

Sexual purity is a prominent New Testament teaching which should be a priority in the life of the Christian. So, what happens if you became a Christian AFTER you had sex or if you were a Christian when you had premarital sex? Or what if you're addicted to pornography or have some other sexual vice to deal with? Can you no longer give the greatest gift of your sexuality, your body, to your future spouse? Are you disqualified from being holy before God? Certainly, not!

I talk about purity and being a virgin a lot with my children; too much, if you asked them. It is critical to me because I want my children to live the best life God has for them. I know from experience that God's ways are best and we don't need to "miss the mark" to learn a lesson. All we need to know is the Word! However, we all have FREE WILL and make our own choices. When I learned that one of my kids fornicated, I was shocked, disappointed and hurt. I may have been a bit angry, too. I did not disown my child; I kept loving him. I felt like he did not deserve to hang out with females, to have any fun or to be in my good graces, because of his disobedience, but I forgave him anyway.

It is true that we don't deserve pleasure since we are born into sin; none of us do. We have all fallen short of His glory and deserve punishment and condemnation. But, thanks be to God, our Father, who SENT Jesus to the cross in our place! Now, those who are in Christ Jesus are not condemned (Romans 8:1)! God is a forgiving God and loves all His children. Yes, He hates the sin, but nothing can separate you from His love.

If you find yourself tarnished by premarital sex, lust, pornography and the like, confess your sin to God and trust that He is faithful and just to forgive you of your sins. If you believe, He will cleanse you from all unrighteousness, and it will be as if the incident NEVER happened (1 John 1:9)! We have an Advocate with the Father – Jesus. God plans to redeem you for Himself, not condemn you. He forgives your sins for His name's sake (1 John 2:12) and desires to be in fellowship with you.

After you have asked for and received forgiveness from God, you must forgive yourself. Don't bring up your past faults; God forgets it and you should too

(Jeremiah 31:34). Decide to never fall in that area and ask for the help of the Holy Spirit to accomplish this task. Store the Word of God regarding purity in your heart. Confess that you are pure, chaste and that your body is set aside for your spouse only. Now, act like it! Do the things that holy, pure people do. Set boundaries and hold yourself accountable for your actions. You are strong enough to do this! The Word of God abides in you, enabling you to overcome evil (1 John 2:14)!

Notes

Meditate

For you were bought at a price; therefore, glorify God in your body and in your spirit, which are God's.

1 Corinthians 6:20, NKJV

I beseech you, therefore, brethren, by the mercies of God, that you present your bodies a living sacrifice, holy, acceptable to God, which is your reasonable service.

Romans 12:1, NKJV

For I am jealous over you with godly jealousy: for I have espoused you to one husband, that I may present you as a chaste virgin to Christ.

2 Corinthians 11:2, KJV

Prayer

Father, God, I desire to please You with my body. Your Word says that You anoint us to stand firm on Your Word (1 Corinthians 1:21). Therefore, I receive Your power to stand firm, unwavering on Your Word regarding purity. Every day I am being transformed into Your likeness (2 Corinthians 3:18), so I desire to be chaste until marriage. Father, may I always want to be pure and help me to remember Your Word so that I don't fall into sin. Thank You, Lord, for Your forgiveness, grace, mercy, and unconditional love. I thank You that nothing can separate me from Your love, in Jesus' name, amen.

Confession

God's Word is powerful. When I speak His Word, it shall not return to me void. It shall accomplish what I please, and it shall prosper in the thing to which I sent it (Isaiah 55:11). I declare I am pure before Christ. I think, act and speak like Jesus. I am holy and pure before Christ. I have given myself to Christ and will honor Him with my body daily. I present my body as a living sacrifice because it is my reasonable service. God anoints me to stand firm in His Word; therefore, I will not waver. I choose not to allow my emotions to control me, no matter what I am faced with. I choose to set my thoughts, feelings, and desires to do the will of my Father.

Day 4: Your Soul

If you've been living for any number of years, you've heard the word 'soul.' Most times, in a church setting, it is interchanged with the word 'spirit.' Are they the same? What is a soul?

The soul is your mind, your will (free will or choice), your intellect, your imagination and your emotions; it is your personality. Your soul is what makes YOU unique. There is no one on heaven, earth, or any planet, like you. Your soul can be likened to your fingerprints; there are no two alike.

Your soul was made by God, for God and made to need God. It is what makes you a PERSON and not a THING. When you accept Jesus as your Lord and Savior, your spirit, which is created in the image and the likeness of God, is made new. You don't get a new one; He completely renovates it! We are three-part beings: spirit, soul, and body. Your spirit is saved once you receive salvation, but it is your job to DAILY renew your soul. Making your soul new, or transforming your mind, is a daily responsibility. Making sure your soul is healthy is extremely important. If your soul is healthy, no external circumstances can destroy your life. If you lose your soul or fail to keep it healthy by renewing it with God's Word, you will succumb to the devices of the enemy.

My daughter was new to the state and to the school. She was shy and had a hard time making friends. A couple of kids said hello, and soon they were talking during recess. After a couple of weeks, she developed her first crush. The little girls ran to tell the boy about her crush on him. Unfortunately, he said some mean things about her beautiful black skin. She was devastated and thought that something had to be wrong with her skin. She CHOSE to believe her external circumstances rather than the Word of God. She dwelled on the situation and the hurt for so long that it became HER truth. She did not read or hear the Word enough to override the negativity. She ALLOWED the voice of a man to be more important than the voice of God.

You need God's presence, His Word and trust in Him to overcome the devices of the enemy. If your soul is unhealthy, you cannot fight against the devil. When you open yourself up to negative thinking and continually dwell on negative emotions, you impair your ability to make godly decisions. Once exposed to these things, the door is open for the devil to oppress you. Oppression shows up as low self-esteem, invalidation, distorted self-worth, fear, social anxiety, suicidal thoughts, and depression.

To keep your soul healthy, you MUST believe God and obey His Word. You do that by renewing your mind with His Word. That means if someone at school or work says something about you that God didn't say, then it's not true. Don't believe it! Be more concerned about what God thinks about you than what your peers think. It means being led by the Spirit of God and keeping your mind focused on life, love, and peace.

Today, she is confident in her beautiful brown skin. Those old memories of mean people making mean statements are a reminder to be kind to all those she meets.

Notes

_____
_____
_____
_____
_____
_____
_____
_____
_____
_____
_____
_____
_____
_____
_____
_____
_____
_____
_____
_____
_____
_____
_____
_____
_____
_____
_____
_____

Meditate

For what will it profit a man if he gains [the approval of] the whole world and forfeits his soul? Or what shall a man give in return for his soul?

Matthew 16:26, ESV

...who by constant use have trained themselves to distinguish good from evil.

Hebrews 5:14, NIV

Do not conform to the pattern of this world, but be transformed by the renewing of your mind. Then you will be able to test and approve what God's will is – His good, pleasing and perfect will.

Romans 12:2, NIV

Prayer

Father God, thank You for saving my soul through Jesus Christ! Thank You for loving me so much that You planned for Your Only Son's death and resurrection so that I, too, could be resurrected with the newness of life. Lord, guide me as I go throughout my day and remind me to think on those things which are true, noble, right, pure, lovely, admirable, excellent and praise worthy according to Your Word in Philippians 4:8. Teach me Your ways and help me to desire Your will. I thank You for safety, love, and peace. Thank You for the mind of Christ and Your wisdom. You have given me all things to enjoy, so I will! I will enjoy life and not be anxious. I ask for Your help to know without a doubt that the Greater One lives in me! In Jesus' name, amen.

Confession

I declare that I think on good, godly things. I have the power to rebuke and cast down all negative thoughts. I do not allow bad things people say to me to dictate how I feel or react. I feel great because God loves me! I want to live, and not die, and declare the works of the Lord. I dwell on the positive and on God's Word. His Word is truth and the final authority in my life! I choose to believe what God says about me, no matter what others say. Fear and anxiety have no place in my life. My mind is strong and healthy; I have the mind of Christ. I am beautiful inside and out. I am smart, loved, important and valued. I am good enough because God created me and His plans for me include success. I choose to have a good day, to be full of joy, no matter what is happening around me, because God has given me the authority to call those things that aren't as if they were! I'm, mighty because the Greater One lives inside of me!

Day 5: Sex, Purity & Dating

In our home, we have a rule which states that you cannot date until you're sixteen, but several of my kids have pointed out friends of friends who were dating as early as middle school. Every home is different and has different rules, but as for me and my house, we will serve the Lord!

Between the ages of 13 and 16, I would teach my kids about purity and end their lessons with some type of purity ceremony to recognize that they are committed to remaining a virgin until marriage. Although it was awkward and uncomfortable talking about sex, negative sexual encounters, and the like with my teens, it was vital for them to understand that situations arise and they should know how to prevent them or escape from them.

My daughter and I were on a field trip at a senior citizen home with her class. As we sang songs with each patient in their room, I noticed a bible on one resident's bedside table. Ms. Angel was a sweet lady who avidly read the *"good" book*. After the other students left the room, she invited us to sit on her bed and talk. Ms. Angel commented on my daughter's beauty and innocence. It made her remember a time in which she was innocent. She warned us both about the importance of being pure for God's glory and gave her experience as proof that she knew what she was talking about.

At 15, Ms. Angel had a boyfriend. He told her all the things she longed to hear and was incredibly kind to her. He made her feel special and unique. They had sex, and she became pregnant. When she informed the boy that she was pregnant, he spoke horribly to her and then abandoned her. She lost her home (her parents put her out of the house), her education (she had to drop out of school) and her CHANCE to attend college.

God created sex for a husband and his wife, and He has reasons why. God is the Great Father who knows all. He knew that Ms. Angel's boyfriend would not stick around to take care of a baby. He knew how broken and hurt that would make her feel. God wants to protect us and keep us from pain just like your parents try to keep you from getting hurt. When you choose to remain pure & chaste before the Lord, you demonstrate that you know that you are extremely valuable, that you understand that your body has been bought with the blood of Jesus and that you intentionally choose to be a holy vessel in which the Holy Spirit can reside.

Besides emotional pain, there are physical consequences to premarital sex as well. There is a very high RISK of contracting diseases that may be incurable and contagious, like AIDS and genital herpes. These STDs can make it nearly impossible or extremely difficult to bear children, cause lifelong health problems and lead to premature death. Remember, God's commands regarding sex are based on His wisdom and divine plan for your life. He wants the best for you and abstaining from sex until marriage is His best plan for you.

The world dangles sex in your face every day; encouraging you to do whatever you want with whomever. But God is a covenant God who wants His children to be in covenant. A covenant is a sacred agreement that brings about a relationship of commitment between two parties, made in blood. A blood covenant is sealed for life and is only broken by death. Marriage is a blood covenant, until death. That is one of the primary reasons why sex is for a husband and his wife. Deciding to remain pure is the first step toward walking out the sanctification that Jesus purchased for you with His blood.

Notes

Meditate

You were bought at a price. Therefore honor God with your bodies.

1 Corinthians 6:20, NIV

I am jealous for you with a godly jealousy. I promised you to one husband, to Christ, so that I might present you as a pure virgin to him.

2 Corinthians 11:2, NIV

So that you may be able to discern what is best and may be pure and blameless for the day of Christ,

Philippians 1:10, NIV

Prayer

Father God, I thank You for purchasing me, redeeming me through Jesus' death and resurrection. Thank You, God, for loving me so much that You planned for my salvation before the foundations of the world. I thank You for blessing me with every spiritual blessing and for giving me the ability to remain firm in my faith (1 Corinthians 16:13; 2 Corinthians 1:21). Today I decided to honor you with my body to demonstrate my gratitude. I have decided to be pure to please You. And because I've decided to remain pure, You enlighten me to discern what is best in every area of my life. Thank You for helping me to abstain from sex until You guide me to my spouse. In Jesus' name, amen.

Confession

I declare that I honor God with my body. My body is the temple of the Holy Spirit, therefore; I will not grieve Him by being impure and sinning against my own body. I will abstain from sex until I am married. I walk pure before God; thus, I can discern what is best for me in every situation I face. I keep myself holy so that I may be pure and blameless for the day of Christ and the day of my wedding. I declare that I am from God and have overcome the world, for greater is He that is in me than he that is in the world. I chose to remain chaste and pure because it is God's desire for me.

Day 6: Sex, Purity & Dating, Part II: The Benefits of Abstinence

Pleasing God is THE ultimate benefit of abstaining from sex before marriage, but there are also other benefits to you. Here is a concise, but essential list of some of the benefits:

Avoid emotional hurt. When you have sex, your soul, body, and spirit are involved. It is a positive, beautiful thing when sex is between a husband and his wife, but can be very detrimental, almost torture, when you have sex with someone who isn't your spouse. Relationships do not always go well, and when sex is introduced into the mix, your emotions get damaged. God wants to protect us from the emotional pain caused by such instances.

Disease-free (AIDS, HIV, syphilis, etc.). There are so many diseases you can contract by having sexual intercourse. This benefit alone can save your life. If you take the time to google images of some of these diseases, I am almost confident that you will flee sexual impurity!

A good reputation. When you "sleep around," you may have an adverse reputation. Even if you happen to escape this side effect of premarital sex, you cannot avoid the fact that YOU have a character flaw which allows you to sin against your own body.

You are aware of your worth. Your body is a precious gift, bought by God, to give to your spouse as a life covenant. That is God's best for your life. He said it isn't good for a man to be alone, so He created a wife for him. You can have confidence that God accepts you.

You can make relationship decisions with your brain and not your body/emotions. You will be pure for your spouse; untainted by other spirits (when you "hook up" with people, you become one with them, meaning your spirit is connected; you get some of whatever spirit is in them).

You escape the penalty for sexual perversion. The Bible lists several sexual perversions and gives examples of the consequences of such actions. Sexual perversion merely is anything besides sex between a husband and his wife.

It is hard WORK abstaining from sex. People may make fun of you, some may not want to date you, or you may find yourself in a situation where you desire to have sex (it's natural). That is why it is important FIRST to decide that you are abstaining from ALL forms of sex until you are married BEFORE you are in real life situations.

When you choose to date, it is best if you date someone who has the same values and morals as you. It is already a task to abstain from sex. You do not want to compound the problem by dating someone who is always pressuring you to have sex. Dating should be about enjoying one another, figuring out how to have a successful relationship, and getting to know the other person to determine if they are a suitable spouse. Don't get it twisted; pleasing God with your body opens doors to all kinds of blessings.

Notes

Meditate

Flee from sexual immorality. All other sins a person commits are outside the body, but whoever sins sexually, sins against their own body. Do you not know that your bodies are temples of the Holy Spirit, who is in you, whom you have received from God? You are not your own; you were bought at a price. Therefore, honor God with your bodies. We should not commit sexual immorality, as some did – and in one day 23,000 of them died.

1 Corinthians 6:18-20; 10:8, NIV

But among you, there must not be even a hint of sexual immorality, or of any kind of impurity, or of greed, because these are improper for God's holy people.

Ephesians 5:3, NIV

It is God's will that you should be sanctified: that you should avoid sexual immorality; that each of you should learn to control your own body in a way that is holy and honorable, not in a passionate lust like the pagans, who do not know God;

1 Thessalonians 4:3-5, NIV

Prayer

Father God, I choose to flee all forms of sexual immorality. I want to please you and be holy like You. Thank You for Your Word which teaches me to control my own body. Thank You, Jesus, for sanctifying me that I may live holy and set apart for You. Father, You, bought my body at a high price and I will honor You by living holy and treating my temple with respect. I choose to wait for sex and give myself to my spouse on our wedding night. Thank You, Father, for the strength to stand firm on my decision. In Jesus' name, amen.

Confession

I declare that my body is holy and sanctified; set apart for my God. I please my Father and avoid sexual immorality; it is my reasonable service for His holy sacrifice for my life. My body is my spouse's gift on our wedding night, and I will not devalue myself by engaging in premarital sex. I reserve all sexual pleasure and gratification to my spouse where the bed is undefiled, holy and pure. I am strong in the Lord and in the power of His might. I am immovable and never tire in my efforts of remaining pure before God.

Day 7: Being Honest

The Bible has much to say about abstaining from lying, not becoming a liar and being honest. In John 8:44, Jesus declared that the devil is the father of lies. If he is our enemy, then we should not be doing anything that he does. It's safe to say that God ALWAYS wants us to be truthful. We are to be like Him, and He cannot lie (Titus 1:2).

We have a saying in our home: liars go to hell. This sassy little phrase was to teach my children to be honest when they were young. It caused some commotion in their early years of school! They would catch kids in a lie, or they heard something that went against the Bible, and they would yell out, "liars go to hell." They argued with kids who said Santa Clause and the Easter Bunny were real. They proclaimed that Halloween wasn't a holiday for Saints. Needless to say, I received several calls from the school.

Although I received calls from their teachers - their attempt to reprimand me for my children's words - it was worth it! My kids knew what a lie was and didn't want anything to do with it. They could quickly recognize the half-truths that the world dished out and they were not going to swallow it. They even helped my situation by broadening the subject to include praying for those who lie, how to persuade a friend to lead an honest life, allowing people to believe the way they want to without condemning them and much more.

It is important to remember that God HATES lies and thus the righteous man should too. We are instructed to stop lying and to be honest, trustworthy and sincere. To be honest, you must be free of deceit and untruthfulness. It means that your intentions and motives are honorable, that you are frank, humble and genuine. If honesty is your lifestyle, people can count on you, and your reputation will be favorable. Not only that, your character will be renowned in your circle of influence.

When you are HONEST, people want to be around you. You're the one people will want to talk to because they know you will tell them the truth. Remember, satan cannot "make" you sin, but he certainly plants the thought of sinning in your mind. YOU must be the one who chooses to be honest at all costs.

God hates lies, so we must RESIST the temptation to lie. Jesus informs us that satan is the father of lies and that the wages of sin are death. Psalms chapter 52 speaks of the enemy's love of evil and falsehood. The book of Proverbs teaches you to be honest and to speak the truth, emphasizing the importance of bringing back truthful reports to those you serve. If you claim to be a Christian, a follower of Christ but fail to follow His teachings, He says YOU are a liar. A liar is also a person who denies that Jesus is the Christ.

Lying is wrong and is something that we all need to avoid. It may seem difficult, at first, to refrain from telling a little "white lie" so that you don't get into big trouble. Or what happens when your friend asks you, "do I look nice in this?" and you don't want to hurt their feelings? Trust God! Rely on Him for the strength, to be honest in a loving way. If it helps, just adopt our little family saying: if you lie, you go to hell.

Notes

Meditate

For the wages of sin is death, but the free gift of God is eternal life in Christ Jesus our Lord.

Romans 6:23, ESV

There are six things the Lord hates, seven that are detestable to Him: haughty eyes, a lying tongue, hands that shed innocent blood, a heart that devises wicked schemes, feet that are quick to rush into evil, a false witness who pours out lies and a person who stirs up conflict in the community.

Proverbs 6:16-19, NIV

The Lord detests lying lips, but He delights in people who are trustworthy.

Proverbs 12:22, NIV

Prayer

Father God, I want to be honest and holy like You. Thank You for strengthening me to do all things through Christ. I ask that the Holy Spirit gently nudge me with reminders to be honest when I am tempted to lie. I pray that I would be reminded that lying is offensive to You. I do not want to offend You or to do something that You hate; therefore, I choose not to lie, in Jesus' name, amen.

Confession

I declare that I am truthful, honest and sincere. I choose to honor the Lord by speaking what is right, noble, praiseworthy and of an excellent report. God delights in me because I am trustworthy. Deceit, trickery and a lying tongue are not a part of my life; I delight in the truth. I enjoy His abundant life and every good and perfect gift. God created me in His image; thus, I do not lie. I choose to be honest, sincere and genuine. I strive to be like my Father; trustworthy in all my promises and faithful in all I do. When I speak, people listen for I have righteous things to say. I open my lips to proclaim what is right. My truth refreshes the spirit of all those that hear. I declare I will speak nothing but the truth in the name of the Lord.

Day 8: What To Do When Things Don't Go Your Way

There will be troubles, trials, temptations, and tribulations in this life on Earth. Jesus told us to expect tribulation and persecution in this world (John 16:33) and to count it as joy when bad stuff happens to us (James 1:2). Bad things happen on the earth because of sin. When Adam and Eve disobeyed God, they allowed a spiritual transfer to take place.

God knows all, even before it happens. He cares for each person, but He gave us all FREE WILL. We can do whatever we want; good or evil. He has given us a gift, not only of life but the ability to decide how our life will be. The authority and ability to make life decisions are in our hands.

God is NOT responsible for evil, death, and hatred! He is the giver of every good and perfect gift (James 1:17). God is the giver of life (Psalm 119:50, John 5:21, Romans 5:17) and the very Creator and Lover of our soul. He has even declared that the last enemy to be destroyed is death (1 Corinthians 15:26).

God doesn't like evil; it is opposed to His modus operandi and His character. He desires for us to choose Him, His way of doing things and reverent obedience to His Son. The decision, however, remains YOURS and He will never infringe upon your free will. So how does this relate to your daily life?

Whenever you run into situations that you don't like, just remind yourself that you control your life; you're responsible for changing your circumstances. It is up to you to ask for His help. You must recognize that there are spiritual principles at work that govern the physical laws that affect every aspect of life.

My youngest daughter is a volleyball player. She was introduced to a club volleyball coach that she liked working with. She tried out for his club volleyball team, but he did not have enough players to create a travel team. She was sad, but I reminded her that God knows best and has other DOORS He can use to answer her prayers. I had been conversing with a Christian volleyball club owner for about three years, and she granted my daughter a chance to tryout at one of her clinics. She not only made the team, but she was also given a full scholarship as well!

We chose to SPEAK what we wanted and stood firm in trusting God. We reminded ourselves that we are responsible for our destiny and the outcomes in our lives. We both decided we were not going to be sad about not being on a club team. We chose to speak what we wanted and expected God to perform His word. Tryouts were over, but He opened another door and granted favor! God is no respecter of persons; what He did for us, He'll do for you! Trust God today.

Notes

Meditate

Truly, I say to you, whoever says to this mountain, 'Be taken up and thrown into the sea,' and does not doubt in his heart, but believes that what he says will come to pass, it will be done for him. Therefore I tell you, whatever you ask in prayer, believe that you have received it, and it will be yours.

Mark 11:23-24, ESV

Know therefore that the Lord your God is God, the faithful God who keeps covenant and steadfast love with those who love Him and keep His commandments, to a thousand generations.

Deuteronomy 7:9, ESV

Count it all joy, my brothers, when you meet trials of various kinds...Every good and perfect gift is from above...

James 1:2, ESV and James 1:17, NIV

Prayer

Father God, I ask for Your wisdom to understand what is happening in the world I live. I thank You for always giving me good and perfect gifts. Because all Your rewards are good, I know when disasters, crimes, and bad things happen, it did not originate from You. Thank You for protecting me from evil by sending me a way of escape. When things are too hazy for me to see the way of escape, I thank You for always going through the valley of the shadow of death with me. You never leave me alone, and I praise You for it! I receive Your strength, joy, peace, and wisdom right now. I access all the benefits You daily load me with by faith, in Jesus' name, amen.

Confession

I am strong in the Lord and in the power of His might. God has provided the way of escape during trials and hard times. He is always by my side; He never leaves me for He is Jehovah Shammah! I am protected under the shadow of His wings, and He surrounds me with a shield. I have the mind of Christ and the wisdom of God; therefore, I know what to do in every situation. I hear the Holy Spirit's voice and follow His instructions. I fear no evil as I walk through the valley of the shadow of death; nothing can harm me!

Day 9: Fighting The Good Fight

When people say, "fight the good fight of faith," what does that mean to you? Well, if your pastor said it, he's referring to using faith in your everyday life. That is very important. The Word says that the just, or righteous in God, are to live by his faith (Habakkuk 2:4; Romans 1:7). Yes, you are to use YOUR faith every day to please God, win your battles and enjoy life. Hebrews 11:6 informs us that it is impossible to please Him without faith, so we must walk by faith daily. However, I'm talking about something more 'down to earth' and natural -- actual fist fighting.

So, you're a Christian. You represent Christ. You ARE the salt of the Earth and the light on the hill. Do you get into fights? What about bullies at school...how do you handle that? Well, Christ was no wimp! If you study the first four books of the New Testament and check out Jesus' life, you'll see that He wasn't timid. Jesus is wisdom and love. Perfect love casts out all fear, so Big Bro wasn't afraid of anything.

He could tell you off, better known as giving you a piece of His mind, without cursing or being disrespectful. He kept it 100 when he called the Pharisees serpents and broods of vipers. He was HONEST when he said that they spoke what was deep in their hearts -- evil. Jesus was throwing out what your parents used to call, "fighting words." Jesus was wise enough to shut down attacks with words and did not have to use his fists. What if you're not that wise and you sense an attack coming your way? What should you do?

My eldest daughter had some haters, as many of us do at some point in our lives. One particular girl in 7th grade made her life miserable. She was afraid of confrontation and felt terrible whenever this girl rallied a group together to bother her. The first time she mentioned the bully, I told her to nip it in the bud before she gathers a crowd. Unbeknownst to me, the group was already forming. Once you have a MOB against you, you need to create a posse to combat the issue. I stepped in and alerted teachers and administration. It turned out that the girl bullied other girls too. The other parents and I, along with the school administration, stamped out her reign of terror via expulsion.

I warned my daughter that she would, unfortunately, face other bullies in life and that she had to LEARN how to stop the hassles before the bully begins to build a team. You must be brave enough to speak out in wisdom, as Jesus did, to send the message that says you're not to be trifled with. What you will say may be different for each person, but something needs to be said the first time you sense a problem. Be quick to stand up for yourself so that people know that you aren't the next victim.

We also have a RULE in our home regarding fights. If you cannot avoid the confrontation and you are hit by someone, you have permission to do two things: either give the person a warning or strike with force to end the fight. A kid kicked my youngest daughter, and she told the teacher. I reminded her that this was the kid's first and last warning. I advised her that the next time the kid hit her in any way, she was to strike with enough force to end the fight. What does that mean? A hit that is delivered with such force that the aggressor has learned not to bother you again.

I can only recall a couple of fights while my children were in school. People know who they can bully and tend to avoid the ones that will put them on their bottom. I taught my children to be peacemaking citizens who will defend themselves and others. Just don't put your hands on them!

Notes

Meditate

You brood of vipers! How can you speak good, when you are evil? For out of the abundance of the heart the mouth speaks.

Matthew 12:34, ESV

You desire and do not have, so you murder. You covet and cannot obtain, so you fight and quarrel. You do not have because you do not ask.

James 4:2, ESV

The Lord will fight for you, and you have only to be silent.

Exodus 14:14, ESV

Prayer

Father God, I thank You for Your protection. I rejoice in You because You are my refuge. Your Word proclaims that You protect me from those that rise against me (Psalm 59:1). You sent help from the sanctuary and continuously give me support from Zion. I receive Your protection and Your support and thank You in advance for deliverance from bullies and all forms of injustice. Holy Spirit remind me of Your protection so that when I'm tempted to become fearful or timid, I have the strength to resist it. Give me the words to say to end quarrels and strife. I ask that You surround me with good friends and people of like precious faith. Thank You for hearing and answering me when I pray. I believe that I receive what I've asked You for, in Jesus' name, amen.

Confession

I am not afraid, for God has not given me a spirit of fear but of love and a sound mind. I am mighty, and my words reflect it. Bullies know I am not a target, and good friends surround me. I am full of compassion and empathize with others; therefore, I defend the weak and befriend the timid. I represent Christ wherever I go and stand tall knowing that God goes before me and is with me. He is my shield, my protector, and my refuge. He is the strong tower that the righteous run into and are saved. I am confident that the Lord saved me and delivered me from all hurt, harm or danger.

Day 10: Politics and Christianity

It seems as if every election is worse than the last. Candidates stretch the truth in HOPES of winning the office sought after while character, integrity, and honesty go out the window entirely. As adolescents, you are bombarded with adults accentuating the importance of being honest, truthful and sincere. I am sure it seems hypocritical when you evaluate many of today's political figures.

People are passionate about specific issues, and politics FALL into that category. Politics and religion are the two topics in which people tend to stay away from if they want to be unified. There is an unspoken rule which says you should not discuss politics or religion at work. It is not a good idea to discuss such topics when just meeting someone, so you don't distance yourself or encourage division, especially for your first impression. But what happens if you and your friend of many years suddenly discover that you're on the opposite sides of the voting booth or don't agree on THE way to Heaven?

Imagine you're in history class and the election was the night before. The school is a buzz, and every teacher is talking about the results. This scenario was Faith's reality. Most of her teachers and peers thought like her, but she was SHOCKED to see a classmate come in wearing a t-shirt supporting the opposite side. Her classmate was proud of the t-shirt and thought everything their candidate did was right. Faith was disgusted and angry when I picked her up from school. She could not believe that this classmate did not agree with her political views and felt as if they could not be friends if they didn't share the same political beliefs.

Being angry will not solve your differences. As Christians, we are to LOVE one another no matter what. Our love is to be like Jesus' love: unconditional. Remember, people will know if we are truly His if we love others as we love ourselves. We can only inspire change when we love people and stand against hate. Standing against hate doesn't mean you're callous to those who spill hatred, it means you commit to praying for them and lovingly dealing with them.

I told my daughter to act as if she never saw her classmates' t-shirt. I encouraged her to treat her classmate the same as if she never knew the classmate supported the other candidate. No matter what people do, we are to treat them with love and respect. Don't get it twisted, we are not to put ourselves in a position to be denied justice or mistreated by individuals, but we are always to love.

So, the next time you find your political or religious beliefs clashing with your peers, continue to treat them with love as if you never knew there was a difference. Your love and acceptance may be the very thing that entices them to open up and hear your point of view, bringing greater depth and intimacy to your relationship.

Notes

Meditate

"You have heard that it was said, 'You shall love your neighbor and hate your enemy.' But I say to you, love your enemies, bless those who curse you, do good to those who hate you, and pray for those who persecute you,

Matthew 5:43-44, NKJV

And you shall love the Lord your God with all your heart and with all your soul and with all your mind and with all your strength.' The second is this: You shall love your neighbor as yourself.' There is no other commandment greater than these."

Mark 12:30-31, ESV

A new commandment I give to you, that you love one another: just as I have loved you, you also are to love one another. By this all people will know that you are my disciples, if you have love for one another."

John 13:34-35, ESV

Prayer

Father God, I thank You for loving me so much and for shedding that love in my heart. Help me to pour the love You have for me out on all those I encounter. Father, I ask that You teach me how to love people who offend me, talk about me or do things that I don't agree with. May I be mature enough to treat them with respect, love, and peace. Thank You for Your Word, Your guidance and Your wisdom that enables me to daily walk in love, peace, and unity with everyone, even when we don't agree with each other. Father, help me to agree to disagree peaceably with those who disagree with me and to forgive those who attempt to use or harm me. Thank You for every spiritual gift in heavenly places and the knowledge to translate those spiritual blessings into manifestation.

Confession

I will agree to disagree with those who don't believe like me. I am guided by the Lord and know how to love those who directly oppose me. I thank You that Your love flows out of me and onto all those I encounter. I love everyone, and I am at peace with all those I meet. I love despite any hatred that I may face.

Day 11: I Like Me

The world is FULL of hurting people. Many times, the cause of the hurt is a lack of love. Jesus gave us a new commandment; to love others as ourselves (John 13:34). Many people read the first portion of this scripture but fail to give the second part just as much weight.

He commanded us to love ourselves! Jesus gave His life so that we could be in a right relationship with God. Jesus loves us that much! The love that motivated Him to die on the cross for us indicates our great value, supreme worth and extreme importance. If He loves you, you ought to love yourself. He thinks highly of you, so who are you to NOT think highly of yourself?

There are a lot of NEGATIVE stimuli that adolescents are bombarded with today. The fashion industry says that you must wear certain clothes, have a particular shape or be a specific weight to be beautiful. Society says that you should be one specific skin color, behave a certain way or do certain things to be beautiful. Social media feeds into the frenzy by echoing the mantra of the day: weigh this much, dress like this, look like this if you want to be beautiful.

With all the commotion, teens construe these constant messages as an indication that something is not quite right — with them. This is a common trick of the enemy; to make you think that you're not worthy or make you loathe yourself. There are girls, and boys, silently hurting inside because they have bought into the trap: the LIE that says they're unlovable. The sad reality is that they have allowed media to skew their perception of themselves; they believe the lie rather than trusting God's truth. Being bombarded with unattainable ideals of beauty perpetrated by the enemy is slowly killing this generation of young folks.

You need to rediscover what it means to be healthy according to God's standards. He is your Creator, and He said YOU are wonderfully made. You are original, a masterpiece created by The Father for His good pleasure. In Christ, you are complete; nothing is missing and nothing broken. He loves us, so that proves that we are worth loving, we are beautiful, and we're important.

If you struggle with your body image or liking yourself, decide today that you will not be tricked any longer. Trust God and believe you are UNIQUE, created uniquely by Him and are worth loving. If the Creator of the Universe loves you, then you *must* be valuable. Search the scriptures on love and learn to love yourself. Confess the Word over your life until you begin to believe it! You are precious, beautiful, and valuable to Him.

If you have given your life to Him, it is imperative that we treat the house we live in (our fleshly body) well because it is where God lives. It is your reasonable service to honor God with your body since Jesus died such a cruel death to purchase your body and free you from sin. Honor God by treating your body well, loving yourself and living a healthy life for Jesus.

Remember, YOU are important to God and loved dearly by Him. You are unique, and there is no one else exactly like you. You are special, one of a kind and cannot be duplicated. If God created you to be all that, then you have the very foundation to like yourself; love the skin you're in! He gave it to you!

Notes

Meditate

For we are his workmanship, created in Christ Jesus unto good works, which God hath before ordained that we should walk in them.

Ephesians 2:10, KJV

For the entire law is fulfilled in keeping this one command, "Love your neighbor as yourself."

Galatians 5:14, NIV

In order that satan might not outwit us. For we are not unaware of his schemes.

2 Corinthians 2:11, NIV

Prayer

Father God, You created me and said that everything You created is good. You showed me Your love by Jesus' death on the cross, and I receive Your love today! Because You love me, I can love myself. Father, help me to like myself so that I can love people like You want me to. Holy Spirit show me how much The Father loves me and how He sees me so that I can think, act, and speak just like Him. If You made me, then I know that I'm good and worth loving. Thank You for teaching me that I am important because I am in Christ. I choose to believe it, right now in Jesus' name, amen.

Confession

I am fearfully and wonderfully made by God. He has deemed me lovable and worthy of His time and attention. God is Almighty and Sovereign and desires to be with me. God loves me and wants the best for me. I am happy with my looks, my body shape, my intelligence and everything else that makes up my personality. I am unique; there is no one on earth like me. God did that on purpose! He created me to be unique and set apart for His works; thus, I am valuable, of the utmost importance, and loved. Because He loves me and has shed His love in my heart, I love others.

Day 12: What Do You Want? (Coveting)

Sometimes there are things we may want, but for one reason or another, we don't have them. It may be the newest pair of shoes, more height, the latest smartphone, a smaller nose, lighter skin or longer hair that you crave. You probably see or know others who possess the things you want. If you're honest with yourself, maybe you feel a certain kind of way since you don't have the THINGS that they have.

As a Christian whose final authority is the Bible, you are not supposed to be jealous of anyone or covet someone else's belongings. To covet means to yearn to possess what someone else has; basically, greed for worldly gain. It is to want and want, never being satisfied. In Exodus 20:17, God tells us NOT to covet. It is idolatry according to Colossians 3:5 and can quickly lead a person to steal, lie, and ultimately murder. The bottom line is, coveting will keep you out of the Kingdom of God!

The Kingdom of God is where we all want to be. In the Kingdom, there is freedom, love, peace, prosperity, healing and everything else you would ever want or need, spiritually, mentally, emotionally and physically. The Kingdom of God is a spiritual system or government; His unique way of operating. *Everyone who receives Jesus Christ, as their Lord and Savior, IS in the Kingdom of Heaven, but all those who are saved do NOT function in the Kingdom of God.* We know this because there are Christians who covet, steal, lie, cheat, and kill.

I can recall several instances where my daughters were sharing the highlights of their school day. The person that spoke ill of them or was rude or had a habit of using profanity later confessed to being a Christian. They were shocked at their confession of Christ because the person acted out of character.

When you encounter Christians that do not ACT like Christ, remember that not everyone in the Kingdom of Heaven will enter the Kingdom of God. They will not live successful, world overcoming lives daily. They will act as if their spirit has not been made perfect; they will act like sinners. They behave this way because they do not take the time necessary to renew their mind with the Word. Do not allow a desire to turn to greed. Do not worry over things you don't have; be content with what you presently have while expecting to receive more.

Let's be clear: there is NOTHING wrong with wanting things just if the desire doesn't consume you. God knows what you want and wants to give it to you, but you must yearn for Him more than anything. Your heart must be pure; it must desire Him above all else. When you want God above all else, He eagerly gives you the desires of your heart just because He loves you. He loves giving you gifts and seeing you happy.

So, there is no need to covet the salary of an athlete, the popular kids' wardrobe or your neighbor's girlfriend. Enjoy what God has given you WHILE you believe Him for your desires. Exercising your faith to obtain a six-figure income, a new trendy wardrobe or a boyfriend is the correct way to get what you want AND experience the safety, love, and success of/in God's Kingdom. Now...what do YOU want?

Notes

Meditate

"You shall not covet your neighbor's house. You shall not covet your neighbor's wife, or his male or female servant, his ox or donkey, or anything that belongs to your neighbor."

Exodus 20:17, NIV

You desire but do not have, so you kill. You covet but you cannot get what you want, so you quarrel and fight. You do not have because you do not ask God.

James 4:2, NIV

Do you not know that the unrighteous will not inherit the Kingdom of God? Do not be deceived. Neither fornicators, nor idolaters, nor adulterers, nor homosexuals, nor sodomites, nor thieves, nor covetous, nor drunkards, nor revilers, nor extortioners will inherit the Kingdom of God.

1 Corinthians 6:9-10, NKJV

Take delight in the Lord, and He will give you the desires of your heart.

Psalms 37:4, NIV

Prayer

Father God, I desire to be pure before You. My spirit is perfect, and I will put in the work to renew my mind with Your Word that my heart may be genuine. Holy Spirit guide me into all truth regarding renewing my mind and daily encourage me to set aside time to spend devouring the Word. Show me the best time and develop my schedule so that I am intentional about renewing my mind and purifying my heart with Your Word. I know that You look at the heart and not the outward appearance. I want You to be pleased with what You see. Father, I submit my heart to You. My heart is in Your hand, Lord, and like the rivers of water, You turn it wherever You wish. In Jesus' name, amen.

Confession

I declare that my heart is pure; I am not covetous. I operate in the Kingdom of God and experience success in every area of my life. I renew my mind on His Word daily, rightly dividing the Word to live like Christ on the earth. I intentionally set aside time every day to read the Word of God. I hide His Word in my heart so I won't sin against Him.

Day 13: Peaceably Agree To Disagree

There are many things that people can disagree on; which team is best, which candidate should win, who's prettiest or who's right. There are roughly 325,145,963 people in the United States as I write this book. That's probably around how many different ideas, thoughts, strategies, etc. that may collide with your beliefs. God made each human being with their own individualized personality, intellect, motives, and ambitions. I can guarantee that you won't even agree with your spouse on every issue all the time!

We are all UNIQUE and special in His eyes. We all contribute something to society. So, what happens when you and your buddy don't agree with which answer is the correct one? There is a proper, godly way to respond and keep your friendship – agree to disagree in peace.

Some people find it hard to accept another person's idea, thought or reasoning when it is different from their own. I think it may be a quest to prove yourself right and the other person wrong. Whatever it may be, if the relationship is worth saving, it is good to know how to agree to disagree with someone without ruining the relationship.

There may be some things that you decide would be a DEAL BREAKER in relationships, especially when dating or just selecting good, quality Christian friends. For example, when it comes to your religion and your spouse, it is imperative that both of you agree on who the one true God is and how to receive salvation through Jesus Christ. It is okay to have friends that are of another religion, but they should not be your closest friend, your BFF. Why? Because whoever you hang around is who you become. We'll talk more about that later (Day 14, page 50).

I recently had a chat with my daughters to demonstrate how you are to peaceably agree to disagree with someone who opposes you or strongly disagrees with you. I was responding to a post on a social media site, helping them to rightly divide the Word of God so they could apply it to their lives. A very cynical person began to call me names and attempted to discredit Christianity. I politely corrected him, purposely saturating my response with love. He came back with another insulting post, and I responded with scripture laced with more love. I blessed him and spoke long life, peace, prosperity, and love over him. I turned the names he was calling me into compliments and his sarcastic comments regarding Jesus' miracles into an ordinary action for Christians.

I explained to my daughters that love conquers hate, even on social media. After I had blessed him over and over and let him know that I had forgiven him for all the names he called me, all he could say was thank you. My girls erupted in laughter, and high fives went around the room. I let them know that whenever they are faced with people who want to oppose them, just give the truth saturated with love. Tell them that you can LOVINGLY agree to disagree with them and forgive them for any wrongdoing or ill will. Your friend will respect you or the relationship may wain away. Either way, you allowed Jesus to shine through you and planted a seed in their hearts. With your prayer, they may open their heart for God to water that seed and one day become a follower of Christ.

Notes

Meditate

When a man's ways please the Lord, He makes even his enemies to be at peace with him.

Proverbs 16:7, NKJV

Agree with God, and be at peace; thereby good will come to you.

Job 22:21, ESV

If anyone teaches a different doctrine and does not agree with the sound words of our Lord Jesus Christ and the teaching that accords with godliness, he is puffed up with conceit and understands nothing. He has an unhealthy craving for controversy and for quarrels about words, which produce envy, dissension, slander, evil suspicions…

1 Timothy 6:3-4, ESV

Prayer

Father God, I read about Jesus when He confronted those that opposed Him. He had such wisdom and restraint while peaceably ending the argument. Lord, thank You for giving me the mind of Christ and the wisdom of God. Thus, I confound the wise and fool alike with my words. Show me how to be at peace with all men, even my enemies, so that I may please You and lead others to You. Show me how to save and cultivate relationships after we have disagreed. When people encircle me with words of hate and attack me without cause, give me the words to speak. I thank You for giving me the power to love those who disagree with me and to bless those who curse me. Holy Spirit teach me how to disagree with others peacefully. Give me witty ways to turn their negative comments into an opportunity to shine Your love on them, in Jesus' name, amen.

Confession

The tongue of the wise brings healing. (Proverbs 12:18). When I open my mouth, I speak words that encourage, comfort, heal and are loving to those who hear them. I will remember that gracious words are like a honeycomb, sweet to the soul and health to the body (Proverbs 16:24). I am at peace with all men and am never hasty in my words. I am slow to speak, quick to listen and slow to become angry (James 1:19).

Day 14: Who Are You Hanging With?

The bible says that bad company corrupts good character in First Corinthians 15:33. That tells me that whoever I hang around, I will end up *catching* some of their attributes. First Corinthians 5:6 and Galatians 5:9 both say that a little leaven leavens the whole lump. Whenever we see a phrase that repeats, it's being emphasized because of its profound importance. These scriptures inform us that whoever you choose to spend your time with has a direct correlation as to whether or not you live a life of character, integrity, and faith.

If you select friends who are mean, lack compassion and belittle others, the chances of you not doing those things DRAMATICALLY diminishes. Even if you don't belittle others and treat them poorly, the mere fact that you hang around such people sends the signal that you not only agree with their behavior, you also practice it.

Legally speaking, if you are with a group of kids and they rob a bank, you are an accessory, even if you were not aware of their illegal activity. You could have waited in the car and never entered the bank, but you will still be guilty. You see, it is a reasonable assumption to conclude that your character is likely the same as the crowd with which you associate. That is why it's necessary to choose WHO you hang with very carefully.

What kind of people should you spend MOST of your time with? Find peers who display godly character. Hang with those that are honest, worthy of your trust and choose to do what's right even when no one is looking. You should avoid those who are rebellious, disrespectful, quick to become angry or those who don't have values like yours.

My daughter was sitting in a crowd with a few acquaintances. One boy said some mean things about one of her friends, whom we'll call Sally. Even though Sally was not present, my daughter said, "Hey!!! That's not nice. She's my friend." The conversation was over. She stood up for her friend. She stopped backbiting in its tracks and proved herself a good friend to hang around.

Sally made a wise choice to have my daughter as a friend. She was smart enough to see all her good qualities which in turn rubbed off on her. As I look back over my youngest daughter's eighth-grade year, I can genuinely say that all the kids in her "group" had the SAME attributes: high GPAs, kindhearted, giving, peaceful, service minded and leaders in the school.

Today I challenge you to evaluate your circle of friends. If you look at the group of peers you hang around, would you say they inspire you to be better than you are now? Does your group of friends have what you want regarding education, ambition, and vision? Are they honest, loyal, and compassionate? Can your peer group teach you something, admonish you when you're out of line or compel you to be your best in all you do? If you answer no to any of these questions, you need to change your peer group. Make a new friend today!

Notes

Meditate

Do not let my heart incline to any evil, to busy myself with wicked deeds in company with men who work iniquity, and let me not eat of their delicacies!

Psalms 141:4, ESV

Do not be deceived: "Evil company corrupts good habits."

1 Corinthians 15:33, NKJV

Prayer

Father God, send good people who have godly morals in my life. May those of godly character cross my path continuously. Help me to recognize those that are not good for me right away. Give me the strategy to peacefully and smoothly slip away from bad influences in my life. May I study Your Word to hide Your ways in my heart so that I may attract good people. Holy Spirit, teach me how to be a good friend and how to draw those who desire to live according to Your Word. I ask for wisdom and instructions on how to get away from those who run towards evil and those who wish to lead me down the broad path of destruction. I am determined to please You in all I do, including choosing who I spend my time with. In Jesus' name, I pray, amen.

Confession

I will not surround myself with evil acquaintances or busy myself with the wicked. I hang with those with a good rapport. I walk in the light as He is in the light and fellowship with those of like precious faith. I discern those who seek evil and stay away from them. I attract those that desire God's best for their lives and associate with those that do His will. I hang with those who are honest, trustworthy, kind, compassionate and holy. My companions help me to be better and do better for the glory of God, and I do the same for them.

Day 15: What Are You Saying?

Did you know that you will have whatever you say – good or bad? There is a Biblical principle found in Mark 11:23 which informs us that whatever we believe in our HEART and speak out of your MOUTH eventually comes to pass. We tend to say things that we think. We express our thoughts and emotions out LOUD all the time. Sometimes we do so, and it gets us into trouble, and at other times, we are much appreciated.

For instance, your sister comes downstairs wearing a hideous fuzzy puke green sweater and her hair is uncombed. You think, "what does she have on" and it almost immediately slips out of your mouth. You spoke your thought, your belief. Your comment will not make your sister feel good about her outfit choice, and it may warrant a comment from one or both of your parents. What about when you see the most adorable baby in the mall. You immediately say, "oh my gosh...your baby is so cute!" That is precisely what you believed and spoke. This time, your comments are much appreciated.

While those are very simplified examples, the same truth may be applied to other situations as well. So, let's apply it to your self-esteem or your ability to excel in math. If you BELIEVE that you are NOT attractive, you will voice that opinion out LOUD. If you believe in your heart that you cannot understand geometry, then you will not be able to succeed in geometry. *Whatever you think about yourself, whether good or bad, you will become.* Whatever you think deep in your heart, you eventually speak out of your mouth.

I have two daughters; they are total opposites. One daughter is bubbly, sociable and adventurous while the other daughter is shy, reserved and cautious. It is inspiring to see how God uses each daughter for His glory in such different ways! However, there was one big difference between them that I would like to change. While one daughter spoke words that created opportunity, hope, and victory, my other daughter spoke despair, fear, and misfortune.

What do you do when you find yourself speaking loss and disheartenment? You change what you say! I created a confession full of courage, fearlessness, accomplishment, and value for her to speak over herself daily! God cannot lie. He is faithful to fulfill His promises, laws, and statues. He established a principle, and He is obligated to uphold it! My daughter used to have bad days because that is what she believed and spoke. As she began to CONFESS otherwise, she planted seeds in her heart for good days. You indeed have what you say! Now, when I ask her how her day went, I rarely hear negative things.

You can have a great day, a great event, and a great life. It's all about what you believe and say. When you fill your mind with good things, you'll be inclined to speak good things. Open your bible and find good things to fill your mind. It will change your life!

Notes

Meditate

For as he thinks in his heart, so is he.

Proverbs 23:7, NKJV

Truly I tell you, if anyone says to this mountain, 'Go, throw yourself into the sea,' and does not doubt in their heart but believes that what they say will happen, it will be done for them.

Mark 11:23, NIV

...God, who does not lie, promised before the beginning of time,

Titus 1:2, NIV

The Lord is not slow in keeping His promise, as some understand slowness. Instead He is patient with you, not wanting anyone to perish, but everyone to come to repentance.

2 Peter 3:9, NIV

Prayer

Father God, thank You for Your promises! I am so grateful for Your love towards me! You love me so much that You've place spiritual principles in the land to benefit me. Holy Spirit, I invite You to teach me how to cooperate with Your laws, principles, and statues that I may live long and prosper. Guide me into all truth and show me Your ways. I ask that I would always be aware of Your guidance and always hear Your instructions. Thank You for not lying to me and for being Truth in my life. Remind me to speak godly things and prompt me to think holy thoughts. I am so grateful for Your assistance and welcome it every second of my life, in Jesus' name, amen.

Confession

I declare that I think, act, and speak like Jesus! I have the mind of Christ and His wisdom. I have whatever I say, and I choose to say good, godly things. I think I am valuable, essential and uniquely created by God; therefore, I am! I proclaim blessings, favor, and life over myself and I see it manifest! I am the head and not the tail! I am above and never beneath. I always win because God has already given me the victory! I am more than a conqueror, and the battle isn't over until I win! God's Word is truth for He cannot lie and He isn't slack in fulfilling His promises. I trust God because He is faithful to perform His Word.

Day 16: What Are You Listening To?

Faith comes by hearing. As a Christian, we hear this phrase a lot but do we really believe it? It has been said that if someone hears something long enough, they begin to believe it. If this is true, it is vital that you only listen to things that will benefit, strengthen and uplift you in a positive manner.

Whatever you hear, forms your paradigm. Your paradigm is like your autopilot; it controls your life. It is the foundation of your thoughts and behavior. Everything you hear, say, see, and read funnels DEEP into your heart. You need to watch what enters your *gates* so that the seeds planted in your heart will yield the type of harvest you desire. If you want success, joy, and wisdom, you need to feed your inner man with the seeds of success, joy, and wisdom. If you feed on profanity, death, and lack, your life will be full of drama, strife, and hostility.

When you take the time to listen to the Word of God, you are increasing your level of faith in specific areas. If you hear the Word on health, you raise your level of faith for divine health, healing and your wellbeing. If you hear the Word on long life, you increase your level of faith for living a long life on this earth. Likewise, if you listen to music that declares that women aren't loyal, are female dogs and thots, you will form a paradigm that causes you to BELIEVE what you are accustomed to hearing.

I remember when my son first started dating. He was so polite and treated his girlfriend well, just as he saw mirrored in our home. Later in college, he started hanging around a crowd of dudes that were not headed anywhere in life. They smoked, drank alcohol and cursed profusely. They were moochers living off his couch. These guys were not ambitious or driven nor employed, for that matter. You become who you hang around! He was listening to these guys and feeding his soul with negative, profane seeds. He eventually repeated what he heard them say. He became rude to his girlfriend and did not act like he was raised in a Christian home.

We were disappointed in our son's behavior, but all is not lost. All ships can be righted once it's known that you're going in the wrong direction. If you're facing a situation in your life that you don't particularly care for, change WHAT you're hearing and WHO you're listening to. Maybe you have a desire to be a positive, successful person but that's currently not the case. If you want a positive, uplifting environment, you need to listen to positive, uplifting, awe-inspiring things!

Do you want to feel great about yourself and be successful? Successful people say successful things, listen to other successful people and feed on successful seeds! I encourage you to surround yourself with positive people and download a bible app on your smartphone to listen to God's Word. Get those seeds of strength, love, and positivity inside your heart and watch your life turn for the better! You hear me?

Notes

_____
_____
_____
_____
_____
_____
_____
_____
_____
_____
_____
_____
_____
_____
_____
_____
_____
_____
_____
_____
_____
_____
_____
_____
_____
_____

Meditate

Consequently, faith comes from hearing the message, and the message is heard through the Word of Christ.

Romans 10:17, NIV

"Now the parable is this: the seed is the word of God….So the Lord said, "If you have faith as a mustard seed, you can say to this mulberry tree, 'Be pulled up by the roots and be planted in the sea,' and it would obey you."

Luke 8:11, 17:6, NKJV

…" This is my Son, whom I love; with him I am well pleased. Listen to him!"

Matthew 17:5 (Luke 9:35), NIV

Prayer

Father, I know that You do NOT listen to sinners, but if anyone is a worshipper of God and does His will, You listen to him according to Your Word in John 9:31. I have declared in my heart and proclaimed with my mouth that Jesus is Lord thus, I am Your child and not a sinner. Thank You for hearing me when I pray. Thank You for my Helper, Holy Spirit. I invite Him to remind me to listen only to those things that are true, honorable, just, pure, lovely, commendable, excellent and worthy of praise. I refuse to listen to gossip, bickering, profanity, backbiting, disrespect, curses, negative commentary, ill will towards others or the like. I invite You, Holy Spirit, to lead me into all truth and show me great and mighty things that will make me strong in the Lord, in Jesus' name, amen.

Confession

I declare that I think of positive, godly things that are pure, just, worthy of praise, honorable and commendable. I will not allow harmful trash to linger in my mind and corrupt my thinking processes. I have the mind of Christ and the wisdom of God; therefore, I think, act and speak like Him. I listen to the Word for He is the beloved Son of God, my Big Brother, and my Best Friend. I plant the seed of God's Word in my heart that I may not sin against Him. Faith comes by hearing and hearing the Word of God. I choose to listen to the Word daily to build my spirit man up, enabling me to think godlike thoughts. I declare I have a sound mind and listen to Him continuously. Amen!

Day 17: Your Thoughts Become Your Behaviors

Your thinking regulates your actions. If you THINK you are inferior to your peers, no matter if your qualifications and accomplishments say otherwise, you WILL be inferior. If you BELIEVE you are unimportant, you will FEEL unimportant. When you feel insignificant, you will not act as if you're an essential part of society; your life won't be valuable to you, and your actions will correspond. You are what you THINK you are, so you need to manage your thoughts accordingly.

You control your mental attitude. How you think determines how you act and how you behave determines how people respond to you. If you're always thinking about negative, unproductive things, you will act accordingly. If you behave negatively, that is precisely how people will react to you.

When encountering people who act maliciously, who belittle others, and sow hatred, we need to understand that sinful nature inspires sinful actions. Without a mind that is renewed by the Word, the sinful nature will only produce negative, ungodly thinking. There will be people, wherever you go, who think, speak and behave maliciously.

The Bible tells us that there will be those who sow discord, are jealous, display fits of rage, are controlled by selfish ambitions, who slander others, who gossip, and create disorder. It is up to YOU to renew your mind so that you are not one of those individuals. You need to believe what God says about you. It is crucial that we evaluate our lives based on the Word, trusting what God says and listening to His voice.

You are the child of The Most High King, so you ARE important, and you should think very highly of yourself. However, you are not to place your worth above anyone else's. God doesn't have favorites; we're all equals in His eyes. You must believe and speak this truth so that your behavior falls in line.

When evaluating our lives, we tend to focus on the behaviors we see in ourselves that we don't enjoy, but we really should be focusing on the thought behind the act. All change comes from a transformation in your thinking. Once you decide to meditate on God's Word daily, the quicker your behavior will line up with what you're thinking.

Thinking the right thoughts lead to the proper behavior, and more importantly, the right character. Take time daily to transform your mind by reading God's Word and thinking on things He would approve. Picture this: if your thoughts were visible and God walked into the room while you were thinking, would He be pleased? After all, God does see your thoughts.

We all want to behave acceptably, but remember, if your thoughts aren't good, your behavior won't be either. Make it a habit of just purposely thinking about things that are pure, of an excellent report, which are admirable, noble, true and right so that your habits, behavior, and character follows.

Notes

Meditate

For I say, through the grace given to me, to everyone who is among you, not to think of himself more highly than he ought to think, but to think soberly, as God has dealt to each one a measure of faith.

Romans 12:3, NKJV

For as he thinks in his heart, so is he...

Proverbs 23:7, NKJV

If anyone among you thinks he is religious, and does not bridle his tongue but deceives his own heart, this one's religion is useless.

James 1:26, NKJV

But I discipline my body and keep it under control, lest after preaching to others, I myself should be disqualified.

1 Corinthians 9:27, ESV

Prayer

Father God, You created me and said that everything You created is good. Lord, help me to be kind and think of myself highly. Father, remind me of Your Word that I may meditate on it daily. As I ponder Your Word, Father, I want to change my mind for the better. As my mind is transformed, my mood and attitude are too. I thank You for enabling me always to have a good attitude and be in a good mood. Lord, I thank You for providing peace, tranquility, and strength to mortify my flesh. I kill my flesh daily so that I act like Jesus. Thank You for Holy Spirit on the inside of me for guidance in living my life for You. In Jesus' name, amen.

Confession

I declare I always think, act and speak like Jesus, even in trials, fatigue, and stressful situations. I know how to conduct myself and keep my body under. I have the mind of Christ, and the wisdom of God dwells in me; therefore, I behave in such a manner that is pleasing to God. I think godly thoughts, stay in a good mood and exhibit a Christlike attitude.

Day 18: You ARE Valuable!

In Genesis chapter one, God created everything and said that it was good (verse 31). He specifically said that we are made in His image (a spirit like Him) and that we have dominion (verse 26). Verse 28 tells us that He blessed us and commanded us to subdue the earth. Chapter two of Genesis shows us that God took His time and gave great care in creating us. God was so intimate with us when He breathed His holy breath into our nostrils giving us life! How awe-inspiring and magnificent to have the Creator of the Universe take time with us. He made us highly intelligent (verse 20) and walked among us (Genesis 3:8). It is evident that we were special to Him.

Guess what? God doesn't change (Malachi 3:6)! We are STILL special to Him! YOU ARE special to Him. His creation IS valuable, and He loves us dearly. He loves us so much that even before the fall of man in Genesis chapter three, He set a plan in motion to redeem us. God gives the first glimpse of His plan of redemption in Genesis 3:15 and fulfills it in Mark 16:6.

The whole purpose of His plan of redemption is to provide us the opportunity to come into His presence rightfully. Why? Because He loves us! He loves us so much that He sent His Own Son to a sin-filled Earth, allowed Him to die and then be resurrected so that we would have the OPPORTUNITY to be with Him. He knew that some people wouldn't choose to come to Him, but He did it anyway! You know what that means? YOU ARE VALUABLE! You are important to God. You are special, valuable, worthy, and a treasure to God!

I want to speak to girls for a moment. We live in a world that says that women are less important than men. Women make less money for the same job as men, and it took a while before we were granted the right to vote in the United States. In other countries around the world, women are treated as second class citizens. A woman's value is only as much as the next man says. Our society purports that the only way to dominate is to use our sexuality. Advertising bombards women with the message that having pre-marital sex with whomever you want is power and gives you worth. It's all a lie; a trick of the enemy!

With such nonsense floating around the airwaves, it is hard for young girls to comprehend their value. The enemy's trick is to diminish Christ's value so that HER value is lost. Many girls are not confident in themselves and rely on men to confirm their worth. The truth is, Christ is The Man and has ALREADY declared you valuable. You are MORE valuable than rubies, diamonds, gold or anything else we deem precious on this planet. You are His greatest creation, and nothing can separate YOU from His love. No matter what you do or say, He will never stop loving you. That makes you valuable, precious and worthy.

Guys, God did not forget about you! He created males first and loved you so much that He did not want you to be alone. God created females just for you! You are special, and He wanted you to live this life with someone special, a female. Be sure you treat women with the utmost respect; they are your equal partner created by God with you in mind. You should always treat women like the JEWEL they are. You should be kind, considerate, loving and patient with women, recognizing their worth in Christ.

If you didn't know before, I hope you see now: YOU ARE VALUABLE TO GOD! You are a stunning creation of God, and He says you are worth more than you can imagine. God made you unique (being the only one of its kind), essential (absolutely necessary; extremely important), and inimitable (so good as to be impossible to copy). Don't allow anyone to tell you otherwise!

Notes

Meditate

I praise You, for I am fearfully and wonderfully made. Wonderful are Your works; my soul knows it very well.

Psalms 139:14, ESV

And God saw everything that He had made, and behold, it was very good...

Genesis 1:31, ESV

For God so loved the world that He gave His Only Son, that whoever believes in Him should not perish but have eternal life.

John 3:16, ESV

Prayer

Father, thank You so much for Your plan of redemption. You redeemed me from the curse of the law, sickness/disease, and death because You love me! Father, show me a facet of Your love every day that I may fully understand and grow closer to You. Holy Spirit, teach me how to love God more perfectly every moment I breathe. May I know my value and worth always. Father, when I'm tempted to feel inferior, ugly, dumb or unworthy, show Yourself strong in my life! Father, I ask for a radical display of Your love for me that will pierce my heart and change my mind and mood! Holy Spirit, illuminate His Word to me so that I understand He has created me to reign on this earth and that I am valuable to Him. If I am precious to Him, I am worthy, important and special. Thank You, Father, for making me special and loving me so much. In Jesus' name, amen.

Confession

I am fearfully and wonderfully made by my Father. What He says is the truth, and His truth supersedes all facts and opinions. God declares that I am precious and valuable to Him; therefore, I am! I will not be moved from His Word concerning me, no matter what others may say. I command respect, honor, and dignity because God made me a royal priesthood and I act accordingly. Everything God creates is good, and I am His best workmanship! I am the head, a winner, more than a conqueror and worthy of His attention, love, and friendship. I am a friend of God; His child and I reign in Christ. He loves me and deems me valuable, special, precious and worthy. I am His treasure, and I will not allow others to treat me any less.

Day 19: How To Make Friends

Middle and high school are very pivotal years. You need a good friend base to be emotionally and academically successful. Friends encourage you, help you study, and tell you the truth. Being surrounded by good friends is of a great benefit to you.

Academics are paramount and can determine a significant portion of your future. However, without sound relationships, your emotional, social and possibly academic, growth will be stunted. Relationships teach you about yourself, your strengths and weaknesses, hobbies and personality. They show you how to fulfill the needs of others and how to select those who will satisfy your needs.

You might be saying that this would be good information *if* you had friends. If you don't have friends or if your current set of friends are not up to par, I have a great suggestion. Extracurricular activities are an excellent place to find friends. All my children played sports and always had a crowd of friends from which to choose.

My sons are football players, and football helped them to cope with our move from Kentucky to California. We made the trek across the country when they were 13 (8th grade) and 10 (5th grade). They were not happy about leaving their friends and having to start anew in their "senior" year of elementary and middle school.

My husband and I made a deal with the boys. We allowed them the opportunity to CHOOSE which football team they wanted to join, if they would "accept" the move gracefully. Our boys had friends immediately, some of which are still in their lives. Their relationships helped them to move forward as residents of California and lessened the longings for Kentucky.

Step out of your comfort zone and use school clubs, church interest groups, and sports as an avenue to build new friendships. There are all kinds of clubs, at school and in the community, from which to choose. There are BOUND to be at least one or two that peak your interests. If you need to make friends, or maybe befriend some new ones, check out your school or community extracurricular activities today.

Meditate

Therefore, my friends, I want you to know that through Jesus the forgiveness of sins is proclaimed to you.

Acts 13:38, NIV

I no longer call you servants, because a servant does not know his master's business. Instead, I have called you friends, for everything that I learned from my Father I have made known to you.

John 15:15, NIV

Greater love has no one than this: to lay down one's life for one's friends.

Joh 15:13, NIV

Prayer

Father God, I ask that You guide me to the extracurricular activity that would benefit me and glorify You. Lord, I pray that the people who are in the clubs or sports that have like precious faith, would seek me out and befriend me. Lord, I ask that You teach me how to sense my friend's needs that I may fulfill them and that my needs may be met as well. Lord, I am trusting the Holy Spirit to lead and guide me in selecting the right friends and treating them like You do. Thank You for Your instruction, in Jesus' name, amen.

Confession

I am a good friend because I treat them just like God treats them. I display love, kindness, and compassion to my friends and in turn, receive the same. I have good friends because the Lord leads me to them and vice versa. I am confident that I will select only the best people to hang around.

Day 20: Refuse To Care About What Others Think

In our social media society, it is so EASY to find out what people think. Opinions are shared so quickly and haphazardly on the internet. And we all know that opinions are not always pleasant. It is very easy to get caught up in the hype of instant notifications and how many "likes" you obtained on your last social media post. However, we must remember that there is only one opinion of us that eternally matters.

God created you, and He knows EVERYTHING about you, down to the unspoken, deep thoughts of your heart. He knows what you're going to say even before you say it and He knows every decision you'll make before you make it! Wow! Our Father God is amazingly awesome! His opinion is the only one that matters, and He's always concerned with your heart.

It is essential that YOU develop your character and attempt to obtain a good reputation. Lots of people think that these two are the same, but they are slightly different. Character is WHO you are while reputation is what OTHERS think of you. God is concerned with your character. When you focus on developing a godly character based on His Word, your reputation has an excellent chance of being excellent too.

There are those instances where the enemy will sway people into speaking ill of you or tarnishing your reputation but you can trust God to defend you. Your job is not to allow other people's opinions of you to define who you are or how you react. Your purpose is to please God in your character by focusing on His opinion of you. If you are busy doing this (focusing on His opinion of you), you won't have time to find out, or care about, what others are saying about you.

Today's devotion is short because I want you to spend TIME meditating. Whatever you meditate on the most, dominates your life. Your mind cannot determine the difference between thoughts and reality, so it is of utmost importance to meditate on godly things to prepare your mind to be renewed. Think about what God says about you and about good things you want for your life.

Search the scriptures and find out just what KIND of character God wants to see in you. Find out what He thinks about you and work on living up to His standards, ignoring the opinions of the world, and you will be sure to experience success.

Meditate

And even the very hairs of your head are all numbered.

Matthew 10:30, NIV

But the Lord said to Samuel, "Do not consider his appearance or his height, for I have rejected him. The Lord does not look at the things people look at. People look at the outward appearance, but the Lord looks at the heart."

1 Samuel 16:7, NIV

Jesus, knowing their thoughts...

Luke 9:47, 11:17; Matthew 9:4, 12:25, NIV

Now the Berean Jews were of more noble character than those in Thessalonica, for they received the message with great eagerness and examined the scriptures every day to see if what Paul said was true.

Acts 17:11, NIV

Prayer

Father God, thank You for creating me and wanting me in Your presence. Thank You for Your high opinion of me! It is so wonderfully awesome to know that You know every detail about me and still love me unconditionally. It baffles me that You keep up with the very number of hairs on my head and that You perfect that which concerns me! You are more than amazing, and I thank You for caring about me so genuinely. Lord, may I remember how much You care for me and place other people's opinions of me in their proper place. Thank You, Holy Spirit, for leading and guiding me in the way of truth and for reminding me of God's opinion of me. It's in Jesus' mighty, matchless name that I pray, amen.

Confession

I declare that I am ONLY concerned with God's opinion of me; opinions of others do not guide my decisions or actions. God is my Father who knows every intimate, unspoken detail about me. He deems me cool, acceptable, lovable and worthy of His concern; therefore, the opinions of others are not material to my feelings, thoughts, decisions, and behavior.

Day 21: Don't Worry, Be Happy

There are a lot of things today that may trigger anxiety, worry, and fear. The Bible tells us that He did not give us a spirit of fear and that we are not to worry but to trust in Him. Whenever God tells us to do something, that means we can do it and that it's His desire that we do so. Thus, to fear or have anxiety is technically a sin.

The enemy is very good at bringing about situations and circumstances that breed worry, anxiety, and fear. It is his JOB to steal your joy, kill your ambition, and destroy your peace. He will bring people or other obstacles to convince you that God won't keep His promises to you and you cannot be full of joy like He said you could.

I have two daughters with two different types of personalities, one introvert, and one extrovert. When my daughter felt anxious about dancing in front of her class for the first time, she bolted from the room in tears. I had to go pick her up from school. Thankfully, we've learned some ways to cope with these feelings while confessing the promises of God over our lives.

When you feel anxious or caught up in worry, just stop and take a deep breath. Taking a deep diaphragmatic breath will stimulate the body's relaxation response. Remember, anxiety, worry, and fear are just feelings, and you can change how you feel with the Word of God.

Take a moment to TALK with God about your feelings. Be sure to remind Him (really yourself) of His promises relating to your current situation. Accept that you are anxious or worried and allow the Word to soothe you into feeling how you want to feel. Talking to God, reminding yourself of His word, empowers you to control your thoughts, and ultimately, how you're feeling.

After you've prayed, confess what you've asked Him for and declare how you feel. Focus on the moment, or a meaningful goal-directed activity, not the future. Focusing on the present moment will improve your ability to manage your situation.

The next time my daughter had to dance in front of the class, she took several deep breaths and prayed before class. She spoke words of victory, triumph, and success over herself as she walked through the classroom door. She succeeded in changing her feelings of worry, anxiety, and fear to confidence, reassurance, and calmness. She was not only proud of the A+ grade she earned in class, but of her ABILITY to take control of her emotions, just like God said she could.

The enemy will do or use whatever he can, including your feelings, to make you think God's Word isn't true. Do not be ignorant of his schemes, attacks, and plots against you! Hide the Word of God in your heart and trust it no matter how you feel. Your feelings are fickle and can be changed. Change your negative feelings with the Word of God and watch your life change for the better.

Notes

Meditate

For God hath not given us the spirit of fear; but of power, and of love, and of a sound mind.

2 Timothy 1:7, KJV

So do not worry saying, 'What shall we eat?' or 'What shall we drink?' or 'What shall we wear?'

Matthew 6:31, NIV

If anyone, then, knows the good they ought to do and doesn't do it, it is sin for them.

James 4:17, NIV

Put on the full armor of God, so that you can take your stand against the devil's schemes.

Ephesians 6:11, NIV

He must also have a good reputation with outsiders, so that he will not fall into disgrace and into the devil's trap.

1 Timothy 3:7, NIV

Prayer

Father God, thank You for Your Word! Because of the gift of Your Word, I am not unaware of the enemy's schemes against me. Thank You for giving me control over my feelings. Your Word supersedes fact, overrides emotion and is the final authority in my life. I receive the power, love and sound mind that You have given me. Holy Spirit, I invite You to show me how to experience all that God has given me and to remind me of the truth: I don't have to worry. Father, I choose to leave anxiety, fear and defeat behind and to trust in You to supply all my need. In Jesus' mighty name, amen.

Confession

I am worry free in Christ. I declare that I have a sound mind, unruled by emotions. I am not anxious or fearful because I trust God to take care of me. He is not slack concerning His promises, and His Word has the power to fulfill His purpose and plans. God has given me the authority to call those things that are not as though they are; therefore, I declare I am free from worry, anxiety, and fear!

Day 22: Obeying Your Parents

Did you know that family is ordained by God? Have you taken the time to sit and think about it; God has designed family for His glory and honor. It is His plan for a husband and wife to have children. It is His plan for a child to have a mother and a father in the home.

The Bible shows us His great plan – family — in the very first book of the Bible. It is His best for a husband and his own wife to have children and function correctly so that all who see them, see His glory. Every person in the family has a role, and each role is essential. We hear a lot taught about the responsibilities and duties of fathers and mothers. There are classes, programs and workshops all focused on teaching parents the best ways to parent their children, but what about the children?

Children have a role in the family, and the Bible did not forget to give them instructions on how to please God in the family. We learn from scripture that children should honor and obey their parents; this is their primary duty. Many think honor and obedience are the same, but they are two different things.

You can HONOR but not OBEY. To honor is to esteem highly, respect, give distinction to or place a high value upon. To obey is to comply with a command, to carry out instructions or behave in accordance with. So, you see, you can respect your parents but not follow through on their instructions.

I have four children, but only three live at home. They have assigned chores on certain days to keep our home clean. They all HONOR me; they esteem my place as their mother daily. However, there are times in which I have been disappointed in their choice to disobey my commands.

My husband and I have rules that govern our home. One of our rules centers on the dynamics of handling instruction; no talking back. So, if I give a task, it is to be performed right then, unless otherwise stated. There is no talking back, whining, negotiating or declining the assignment. When my children fail to complete the task or fuss under their breath while finishing it, they disobey God and me.

As Christian children, you are to honor AND obey to please the Father, no matter if you feel like doing it or not, no matter your age. God says that obedience is BETTER than sacrifice. He even equates love with obedience. Jesus went on to say that we show Him that we love Him when we obey His commands.

Jesus is our example. He obeyed EVEN until the DEATH of the cross (Philippians 2:8). It was evident that Jesus didn't want to endure betrayal by His friends, pain, and death – that's why He asked Father God if the "cup" could be removed (Luke 22:42). He honored AND obeyed His Father by submitting to His authority and completing the task in love (John 19:30). Honor AND obey your parents daily by respecting their authority AND following their directions. You will please them, your God and enjoy long life on the earth.

Notes

Meditate

Children, obey your parents in the Lord, for it is right. Honor your father and mother – which is the first commandment with a promise - so that it may go well with you and that you may enjoy long life on the earth.

Ephesians 6:1-3, NIV

If you love me, keep my commands.

John 14:15, NIV

Children, obey your parents in everything, for this pleases the Lord.

Colossians 3:20, NIV

…To obey is better than sacrifice, and to heed is better than the fat of rams.

1 Samuel 15:22, NIV

Prayer

Father God, I want to please You so that I will honor and obey my parents. Lord, thank You for Holy Spirit and His guidance into all truth. Holy Spirit, teach me how to properly honor and obey my parents while I please my Father. When I am tempted to ignore my parents' instructions, bring back to remembrance that obedience is better than sacrifice, in Jesus' name I pray. Amen.

Confession

I please the Father by honoring and obeying my parents. I receive long life on the earth as an immediate reward for pleasing You. I declare that I will honor my parents as well as obey their instruction. I speak life, wisdom, and health over my parents and declare that they have the mind of Christ. I am sure to carry out the instructions of my parents and do so in a godly manner.

Day 23: Who You Represent?

As a child of God, you are to represent Christ in everything you do. You should be the best student in the class, the best team player, the best dancer, the best at whatever you choose to do. Your conduct should be holy, godly and excellent always. Why? Because He is Excellent and we represent Him on the earth. When people encounter YOU, they are having an encounter with the Father. We are His hands and feet on the earth. We are the salt and the light on the earth. We are His ambassadors.

Every day we are to do our very best in whatever we set out to accomplish. We are commanded to do all for the glory of God, so every decision counts. Our choices determine our behavior; thus, we need to be full of the Word of God to make sound, godly decisions despite our feelings. Therefore, it is vital to do your best with any project or activity in which you are involved.

No matter what you are involved in – homework, gym class, geometry, football or violin recitals – give ALL your time, energy and effort in completing the task to the best of your ability. Commit yourself to excellent results and God will honor your attitude of excellence.

I recall my youngest daughter telling me about her biology class and all the shenanigans that happen daily. There are a group of boys who are rowdy and like to push everything to the limit. They all know she's a Christian and, just for fun, attempt to rattle her with their questions. They ask her how she knows that there's a God and presses her for evidence. They picked the wrong girl! She ran down a list of examples from her life, in her sweet, patient manner, that left them speechless.

They chose to pick on her because she is always kind, full of joy and helpful. Several people have asked me, "Is she *really* joyful *all the time*?" Yes! The joy of the Lord really IS her strength! When people see you walking out what you preach, they will test you to see if you are committed, diligent and sincere. If you choose NOT to be the best you can be, it will show, and your fault will prevent someone from coming to Christ.

It is a joyous feeling to lead someone to Christ! If you have never led someone to Christ, you're missing the best high on earth. It is a feeling like no other, and it starts with a commitment to be excellent at whatever you do. You represent something or someone every time you act. Your decisions determine who or what you represent, good or bad.

So, who you represent? If you told someone that you are a Christian would they be surprised? Do your actions resemble Mother Theresa or Adolph Hitler? You can say you belong to Christ, or you're a good person, but we all know that actions speak louder than words. Who are your actions imitating?

Notes

Meditate

So whether you eat or drink or whatever you do, do it all for the glory of God.

1 Corinthians 10:31, NIV

We are therefore Christ's ambassadors, as though God were making His appeal through us. We implore you on Christ's behalf: Be reconciled to God.

2 Corinthians 5:20, NIV

We put no stumbling block in anyone's path, so that our ministry will not be discredited.

2 Corinthians 6:3, NIV

Prayer

Father God, I want to do and be the best for Your glory and honor. Lord, show me how to live an excellent life. Holy Spirit I invite You to guide me; I open myself up to You. Father, speak to me in a way in which I will hear and understand. May I be attentive to Your voice and always choose not to follow the voice of the enemy. Give me step by step instructions on how to represent You in whatever situation I find myself. Holy Spirit remind me that I am the Father's ambassador so that all I do may please Him. May my conduct be excellent so that I am not a stumbling block to those outside the body of Christ. Lord, give me the exact words to speak to all those I encounter so that I may have the privilege of leading them to You. In Jesus' mighty, matchless name, amen.

Confession

I am Christ's ambassador, and I represent Him on the earth. I make a conscious effort to not be a stumbling block to others. I represent Christ well. I walk upright, according to the Word of God. I am not moved by my emotions; I walk by faith. I excel at whatever I put my hands too so that I may give God glory. In every area of my life, in whatever I am doing, I will give my best effort since my Father is watching. Those who have served well gain an excellent standing and high assurance in their faith in Christ (1 Timothy 3:13). Since my Father has already prepared good works for me to do before the foundations of the earth, I will gladly excel in everything, doing good which pleases Him (Hebrews 13:16).

Day 24: PMS (Controlling Your Emotions)

Well apparently, this section is for females, but males may learn a thing or two from reading this as well. We all know a woman who is extra - extra mean, extra grumpy, extra sensitive, extra irritated and extra mad – during a specific time of the month. It could be your mom, your aunt, your best friend...even YOU. If you haven't met a female-controlled by PMS, you've seen her portrayed on TV sitcoms. On TV, it is funny to see a lady flying off at the handle because she's controlled by her emotions. In reality, it is an unfortunate event.

Living on earth requires relying on your senses, your emotions, but in the Kingdom of God, we are to rely on faith. In the Kingdom of God, emotions are our ENEMY. Feelings and emotions are fickle, can be manipulated, and change frequently. Faith is constant, guaranteed, and absolute truth.

You experience victory over your emotions by being LED by Holy Spirit. If you allow Holy Spirit to guide, control and rule you, you will walk in truth, integrity, and peace. Those who are LED by Holy Spirit are mature Christians. Mature Christians diligently follow the desires of the Spirit of God and NOT their fleshly desires.

To mature in Christ, you need to digest the Word DAILY. You will know what is acceptable and pleasing to God, for the Word is His will. Feeding your spirit man on the Word of God every day gives you the tools and ammunition to live a life of integrity and victory. Knowing God's will up front makes deciding a whole lot easier. If you already KNOW that the very appearance of wrongdoing is a sin, then it is easier for you to stay clear of shady people, events, and activities to eliminate the chances of something looking wrong in anyone's sight.

Controlling your emotions takes dedication, commitment, and patience. You must CHOOSE to do what the Word of God says rather than acting on how you feel. That's hard! When you're tired or annoyed, it's difficult to remember what the bible SAYS about your situation and then ACT on it. That's why it is imperative that you are full of the Word of God. Remember your SOUL (your mind, will and emotions) runs subconsciously, like an autopilot. Your SOUL needs to be synced with your recreated spirit man in order for your "default" responses to be Christ-like. So, when you're full of the Word of God, your unconscious behavior, thoughts, and attitude — your DEFAULT — IS the Word of God!

Whether you're suffering from PMS or everyday fickle feelings, decide TODAY to commit yourself to STUFFING your soul with the Word! Choose to act on the Word of God when you're frustrated, sad, irritated, angry, or whatever. Be patient with yourself but demand dedication; hold yourself accountable. Each time you choose to act on the Word rather than your feelings, the easier it becomes the next time. Remember, your actions tell the world who you represent!

Notes

Meditate

The Lord will guide you always; He will satisfy your need in a sun-scorched land and will strengthen your frame. You will be like a well-watered garden, like a spring whose waters never fail.

Isaiah 58:11, NIV

For those who are led by the Spirit of God are the children of God.

Romans 8:14, NIV

Prayer

Father, I know that whatever I ask, I receive from You because I keep Your Word and do those things that are pleasing in Your sight (1 John 3:22). Today, I come asking for Your help in acting on Your Word when I am frustrated, irritated, suffering from PMS or whatever. I thank You for giving me a spirit of wisdom and understanding. I have the mind of Christ so I can make the right decisions concerning everything I face in life. Thank You, Lord, for guiding me continually and satisfying my soul in drought. Thank You, Holy Spirit for teaching me how to delight myself in the Lord. I am not moved by what I see and speak the Word no matter how I feel. I can do all things through Christ. In Jesus' name, amen.

Confession

I am led by the Spirit, not by my feelings or emotions or other people's opinions. I hear from God; I know my Father's voice and the voice of the enemy, I choose not to follow. I make godly decisions and yield to Holy Spirit's guidance. I choose not to allow my emotions to control me, no matter what I am faced with. I am in control of my feelings, and I choose to have a great attitude, godly thoughts and behave in a Christ-like manner no matter how I feel. I am patient; constant, never changing my convictions, even during trials, adversity or fatigue. I choose to set my thoughts, feelings, and desires to do the will of God. I expect the words I confess to sink into my spirit and prosper my life, for God watches over His Word to perform it!

Day 25: Social Media

It is amazing how essential social media is for young adults. There are unspoken, unwritten rules about following people on Instagram, specific meanings behind how many likes your posts garner, and the vast importance of the aesthetics of your feed. Technology can be a beautiful thing or a colossal nightmare. If you're not careful, you can get sucked into the artificial acceptance and self-esteem lowering mindset that comes along with our technologically social society.

Don't get it twisted; I love my social media! I just write my own rules and understand that my IG account is only for my enjoyment and entertainment. I do not focus on how many likes my post has or who did or did not follow me, the total number of followers I have or anything else. I use it for my own purpose: to display the best parts of my life.

Social media can be entertaining and very enjoyable, but most often I hear of teens being affected in negative ways. Experts say that teens have more anxiety and less confidence in themselves due to extensive use of social media. Staying on your smartphone and browsing social media sites, prevents the younger generation from learning CRITICAL social skills. Social skills are essential in forming and maintaining relationships as well as building self-confidence. Without real-life relationships, you lack the opportunity to practice relating to people, getting your needs met and learning how to meet the needs of others. I believe that is why it is so easy to bully others on social media; there's no *real* relationship connection. Empathy is lacking in the younger generation because you CANNOT learn that from a screen.

Social media can also negatively impact your time. You can EASILY get caught up in connecting with your followers or scrolling your feed for hours at a time. Spending significant amounts of time on social media prevents productivity and sound sleep. Parents are most concerned about **imposters**; evil people who claim to be your age but have sinister ulterior motives instead.

Your parents can talk to you more about those issues; I want to focus on what I call the **comparison factor**. Peer acceptance is a big thing at your age, and a lot of times it drives what you do, whether good or bad. A lot of females, males too, compare themselves to the images they see on social media. It is crucial that YOU know that YOU ARE VALUABLE and unique in your own right. God made YOU unique (being the only one of its kind; unlike anything else), essential (absolutely necessary; extremely important) and inimitable (so good or unusual as to be impossible to copy). You may see qualities in others that you desire for yourself but NEVER crave them so much that you dislike yourself, or the person to which you compared yourself. That is self-destructive and diminishes the light God placed inside you.

If you are feeling insecure about yourself, you WILL NOT feel better if you belittle others. It will only make you feel worse and create a downward spiral that is hard to escape. You do not have to spend hours pruning your online identity to create the perfect you. Most of all, do NOT allow your social media feed to place pressure on you to be like someone else. You need to learn to feel good about yourself.

Feel good by focusing on what you do well; your good features, and all the other good things about you. If you can't think of anything good, ask your parents or someone you call a friend. I am confident that those who care for you can run down a LIST of things they love about YOU. Let that list boost your self-esteem and fill your social media feed with that!

Notes

Meditate

I praise You because I am fearfully and wonderfully made; Your works are wonderful, I know that full well.

Psalm 139:14, NIV

But you are a chosen people, a royal priesthood, a holy nation, God's special possession...

1 Peter 2:9, NIV

Therefore, as God's chosen people, holy and dearly loved, clothe yourselves with compassion, kindness, humility, gentleness and patience.

Colossians 3:12, NIV

Prayer

Father, thank You for choosing me, dearly loving me and creating me to be like no other. You made me in Your image; therefore, there is no one like me. I am the only me, and You are well pleased with Your creation. Holy Spirit, when I don't feel good about myself, I invite You to remind me that I am royalty, God's exclusive possession, fearfully and wonderfully made by Him for good. Teach me not to compare myself to others, realizing that we were all created to be different with unique gifts, talents, and personalities for Your glory. Father teach me to respect and celebrate the differences that make each person unique while enjoying and appreciating what makes me unique. Lord, help me to enjoy social media and not yield to the temptation of comparing myself to images I see on my feed, wasting valuable time and sleep or using my social media platform to harm others. Thank You for showing me how to use my platform to uplift and edify those who scroll past it. In Jesus' name, amen.

Confession

I like myself and value my unique qualities that define my personality. I celebrate the differences I see in others and am careful not to compare myself to the images I see. My social media platform is entertaining, fun and uplifting. I will not belittle, berate or demean others via social media. I empathize and pray for those that are hurting and speak life over them. I use my time wisely and escape the trap of empty web/social media feed surfing. I am safe on the internet and allow Holy Spirit to lead and guide me while surfing. I am fearfully and wonderfully made and remember that there is a real person, a person that God created and loves, behind each social media account I come across.

Day 26: The Good Employee

As I write, it is approaching the holiday season. The weather is cooling, and almost every retail store has a "Help Wanted" or "Now Hiring" sign posted. In the next couple of weeks, college kids will be home from campus and grade school kids will go on winter break.

Winter break is always a good time to get a job and put a little extra cash in your pocket if that's something you want to do. Maybe you're not in school or already past that stage in your life, and you are already employed. If you were the boss, would YOU hire YOU?

A GOOD employee is one that is reliable and trustworthy. Being trustworthy and dependable means that you can be trusted to show up at least fifteen minutes before the start of your shift as well as complete your assigned task to the best of your ability without supervision. You can depend on an excellent employee to be committed to their work and expect them to *follow through* almost always.

A good employee is also accountable or responsible for their own actions. He or she does not blame others for their shortfalls and is eager to quickly correct mistakes. The *work ethic* of a good employee is impeccable and shows their willingness to do more than just clock in and out every day.

A good employee is also a TEAM player and is accustomed to giving and receiving constructive feedback. An employer wants to hire employees that are encouraging, have a positive attitude and naturally boost the morale of their co-workers.

My eldest son has an impressive work ethic. He is dependable, punctual, organized, a team player, and always impacts his environment for the better. Everyone loves working with him, and employers like to hire him. He learned his work ethic from his dad, a hard worker who strives to complete his tasks in excellence. The fuel behind the zeal to obtain a great work ethic is MORE than just to be considered a good employee.

My husband works hard and strives to be the best because he is a representative of Christ on the earth. Because he is dependable, when he speaks with others about God, they can receive the truth that God is trustworthy. My husband works, not for his employer, but for his God. When he is striving to please his God, he surpasses the expectations of his employer.

Jesus promised that we would encounter tough times in this life and that includes on your job. There will be dangerous situations and adverse circumstances in every area of your life, but you are expected to handle it appropriately. How? By continuing to be a good employee – no matter what you face. When you are honest, dependable and trustworthy, even if a co-worker lies on you, you will still come out on top. God promises to make even your enemies at peace with you when YOU continuously do what's right in His sight.

So how about you? Do you have these characteristics? If not, make it a point to incorporate them into your life today.

Notes

Meditate

Whatever you do, work heartily, as for the Lord and not for men,

Colossians 3:23, ESV

Agree with God, and be at peace: thereby good will come to you.

Job 22:21, ESV

When a man's ways please the Lord, He makes even his enemies to be at peace with him.

Proverbs 16:7, ESV

Prayer

Father God, I always want to please You in whatever I am doing so I have an opportunity to tell others about You. Lord, I ask that You help me develop the qualities of a good employee. Holy Spirit, remind me of how the Lord wants me to treat others, put their needs ahead of mine and do things in its proper order. Father, I receive Your strength to put forth effort into the tasks that I may complete them in excellence. May my work ethic be known and place me before great men that I may have the opportunity to give You the glory. In Jesus' name, amen.

Confession

I declare that I am dependable, reliable, punctual, and accountable for my own actions. I am a thinker and strategically plan how to complete the task before me successfully. Whatever I decide to do – classwork, sports, exams, cleaning, research paper, wash the car, build a house — I will do it as if God Himself asked me to do it for Him. Whatever I put my hands to prospers. I am organized, self-motivated and work well with teams. I am prepared and have taken the necessary time to master my profession. I am a good employee and am desired by many employers. I declare it so, in Jesus' name!

Day 27: Church & Bible Study

When Jesus walked the earth, He established the church before returning to Heaven. He stressed that He was the foundation of the church and that He is the head. The church is not the building, but the people of God and He is the leader of us all.

There is great persecution against the church, now and at the beginning (Acts 8:1). We are to be a body functioning as ONE, residing in peace, building up one another. The church building is where the followers of Christ gather to learn how to reverence the Lord and be lead by the Holy Spirit. The church is where you receive instruction on how to live a godly life, where you worship God as one. The purpose of being built up is so that saints are equipped to make known the manifold wisdom of God.

Saints make the manifold wisdom of God known by feeding the hungry, clothing the naked, caring for the widows and fatherless, seeking/saving the lost, and loving their neighbor. Studying the Bible, in church and at home, equips followers of Christ to successfully fulfill His commission. The church, the body of Christ, is to be presented to Christ in splendor, without spot or wrinkle, holy without blemish. He established the church to give us the support and training necessary to get the job done.

When my children were younger, they had NO choice when it came to church attendance. I was the choir director in one service and on the praise team in two other services. We attended church four times on Sundays plus every Wednesday and Thursday. After moving to California, our attendance has dwindled to just once a week. As the kids matured, they gave *excuses* why they *couldn't* make it to church on Sunday.

Church services may seem boring to you and, like my kids, you don't like the youth/young adult group, but it is still important for children of The Most High God to gather together. Remember, if you call yourself a Christian, your life's goal is to please God. There is no better way to please The Father than by putting your "religion" into practice. It's vital that we hear the Word from our leaders (pastors, apostles, prophets, evangelists, etc.). We are to consider the outcome of their way of life and imitate their faith.

When my children choose to obey me, repay those who harm them with love, and transform their thinking to align with Christ's ways of doing things, they PLEASE Him. You are benefited by attending church whenever you can, in this life AND the next.

Church and bible study are two ways we learn HOW to become disciples of Christ, which fulfill the 'great commission' and attains our life's purpose – pleasing God. The next time you don't feel like attending church or reading your bible, think about your RELATIONSHIP with God. Remind yourself that your life's goal is to please Him and you learn HOW to please Him by spending time hearing and reading His Word.

Ask God to give you a revelation on WHY He wants YOU in church. Ask Him what ROLE do YOU play in the local church body. Take a moment to sit alone with God and listen to Him. Now, write down what you sense Him saying.

Notes

Meditate

Not forsaking the assembling of ourselves together, as is the manner of some, but exhorting one another, and so much the more as you see the Day approaching.

Hebrews 10:25, NKJV

How, then, can they call on the one they have not believed in? And how can they believe in the one of whom they have not heard? And how can they hear without someone preaching to them?

Romans 10:14, NIV

And I tell you, you are Peter, and on this rock I will build my church, and the gates of hell shall not prevail against it.

Matthew 16:18, NKJV

Do your best to present yourself to God as one approved, a worker who does not need to be ashamed and who correctly handles the word of truth.

2 Timothy 2:15, NIV

Prayer

Father, I know the church is important to You. I am part of the church, so I am important to You. I thank You for sending Christ to establish the church, to redeem my life and to give me abundant life, now and forever. Lord, I ask that You give me a revelation that I may more clearly understand just how crucial it is to You for me to meet with the Saints on a regular basis. The Bible tells me of Your desire for the body of Christ to be unified, making it a habit of meeting together to worship You. Thank You for more revelation in this area, in Jesus' name, amen.

Confession

I will not forsake assembling with the Saints. It is important to work as one so that we effectively lead the lost to You. I declare that I give God joy gathering with the Saints, having the same mind, the same love; in one accord. When the Saints assemble, there is a corporate anointing that strengthens and uplifts; even the very gates of hell cannot prevail against us.

Day 28: Family Over Everything

As I'm scrolling through my social media feed, I see lots of hashtags. One of the most popular ones relating to the family is #FOE. It's usually coupled with photos of families spending time together, doing something cool or just hanging out. This hashtag expresses that we will do ANYTHING for our family because we genuinely care for them.

Some people would fight, kill or die for their family members. The family is even the theme of some of our most popular movies. When you read advice columns, they always speak to taking time for your family and mention that that is what's TRULY important. Studies show that Americans rate family and health as the two most important aspects of life and happiness.

God is all about family. In Genesis, we see that the first command He gives is primarily to create a family. When Jesus walked the earth, He spoke of God as The Father, our Father. The family is essential to God, and that is why the enemy wants to destroy families.

The family is about LOVE and support, a lifelong commitment. Families show love in many ways: supporting your endeavors, servicing your needs, assisting you in numerous capacities. One way we show one another our love is supporting them at their functions. My boys played football, and my girls ran track and cheered for our local youth league. Our family outings consisted of supporting each child at their games. If one daughter's lunch account were zero, the other daughter would share her lunch. If one son forgot his jersey, the other son would give up his.

Those examples are some simple ways that my children displayed their LOVE for one another when times are good. What about when times are bad? When family members are angry with one another, are fighting or are being harmed by outside people or circumstances? You do the same thing: love.

When my younger son was a teenager, he had issues with authority. He was very rebellious and most often did not follow instructions from adults, including me. There was a day that we were yelling in each other's face, saying things we wish we would have never said to one another. After our anger subsided, we both felt terrible about the situation. Later, we had a rational conversation which included apologies.

Even when you disagree with someone or dislike what they have done, you can still show your love for them. This very display can be the thing that bridges the gap and removes the anger or hurt you feel. When you do this, God promises that your home will stand (during bad times) and that there will be much treasure (lots of good times & memories).

Now that my son has matured, there are no more arguments. We may disagree, but there is no yelling. We have both learned how to express ourselves without anger and practice showing our love to one another on a consistent basis.

Even if everyone in your family isn't saved (committed to following Christ), your love can still be the very thing that allows you to gain an opportunity to lead them to Christ. Today, make the conscious decision to LOVE your family, and everyone else, the way God commands. Not only will you please God, but you will reap many wonderful benefits in your family and every other area of your life.

Notes

Meditate

because, if you confess with your mouth that Jesus is Lord and believe in your heart that God raised him from the dead, you will be saved. For with the heart one believes and is justified, and with the mouth one confesses and is saved.
Romans 10:9-10, ESV

---

who desires all people to be saved and to come to the knowledge of the truth.
1 Timothy 2:4, ESV

To give His people the knowledge of salvation through the forgiveness of their sins,
Luke 1:77, NIV

The Lord is near to all who call upon Him, To all who call upon Him in truth.
Psalm 145:18, NKJV

So they said, "Believe on the Lord Jesus Christ, and you will be saved, you and your household."
Acts 16:31, NKJV

Prayer

God, Your Word says that if I confess with my mouth and believe in my heart that You raised Jesus from the dead that I would be saved. I believe that You are God and Jesus is Your Son Whom You raised from the dead; therefore, I am saved. Father, since it is Your heart that all men be saved, I take it upon myself to plant the seed in the hearts of all those I meet, including my family. God, I thank You for watering the seed and allowing me to work alongside You in reaching the lost. Thank You for delivering my relatives from every evil work and preserving them for Your heavenly kingdom. I claim my family, friends, and coworkers (classmates) for Your kingdom. Father, Your Word implies that if I make You the foundation of my family, we will be blessed. I dedicate my family to You and declare all my family members saved. As a member of the (INSERT YOUR LAST NAME) family, I vow to love them as You do. Thank You for helping me to be loyal, respectful and honorable towards all members of my family. Father show me how to end strife, keep calm, be peaceful and wise when dealing with my family members. Holy Spirit guide us in all that we do and teach us to laugh together, bear each other's burdens and forgive one another, in Jesus' name, amen.

Unsaved Family Confession

Father, in the name of Jesus, I come before You in faith, believing I receive what I ask for at the moment I pray. It is written in Your Word that You desire that none should perish; therefore, I bring (INSERT YOUR UNSAVED LOVED ONE'S NAMES) before You this day. Satan, you are bound from any demonic activity or influences against (REPEAT THEIR NAMES). Their spirits are set apart for God's use. Father, use me, as Your laborer in their path to bring words of comfort, healing, and salvation that is so simple and full of love that they cannot help but to listen, receive and accept. Thank You for delivering them out of darkness into Your light. I choose not to have a lazy, lukewarm, wimpy, apathetic spirit. I will press in and stand in the gap for them. Thank You for enabling me to endure with patience and joy until the manifestation. Help me to see them as You see them: complete in You — in church, serving and loving You. No matter how long it takes, I will not allow the devil to abort my dream and vision of seeing all my loved ones saved, filled with Your Holy Spirit, healed, in peace and prosperous. I am patient to see the victory come! This is my confession of faith, in Jesus' name. amen.

Who I'm Believing God For

_____
_____
_____
_____
_____
_____
_____
_____
_____
_____
_____
_____
_____
_____
_____
_____
_____

Day 29: How Can I Talk To God If I'm Living In Sin?

If you or your loved ones were to die TODAY, do you know if you would be with God or be punished forever in hell? That's a sobering question but make no mistake about it, God wants ALL men to be saved! Everyone has heard John 3:16 which emphasizes His love and intent for mankind. It's astounding to know that The Creator of the universe planned for His Own Son to satisfy our debts – with His death and resurrection — so we could be reunited with God; free from sin. It will take us our entire lives to REALLY comprehend such agape love, but we can surely cash in on the benefits now!

Sometimes people lose their way and yield to sin. The devil is a trickster; he makes sin look like FUN. However, the truth is that the wages, or consequences, of sin, is death, so it's up to us to take precautions against sinning and practice a "sin less" life.

So, say you do fall into sin, what then? When my oldest son attended college in Arizona and faced lots of opportunities to yield to sin. He didn't always choose to do what's right. Because of his wrong decisions, he felt that he could not talk to God. He believed that since he wasn't living "100% in His image" that he forfeited his right to speak to God. THAT IS A LIE FROM THE DEVIL.

In the church world, we hear clichés like, "you can't live in sin and still serve the Lord" and "you have to be hot or cold" which are derived from scripture but don't necessarily express the overall principle behind the verse. So, although these sayings are based on "a truth" in scripture, and are used to encourage followers of Christ to fulfill that truth, these church clichés can mislead Christians causing frustration and an eventual straying from God.

My son thought he had no RIGHT to speak with his Father, no claim to His throne and felt devoid of His presence. This is not only untrue, but it's also a common trick of the enemy. It is important to remember that children of the King have an advantage, a privilege, over the world- they are saved. Salvation is predicated on YOUR belief and faith in Jesus' death, burial, and resurrection.

There are many ways to sin, and all sin leads to death, but there is only ONE sin that is unpardonable- blasphemy against Holy Spirit. Even Jesus did not come to earth to condemn mankind; man condemns himself when he rejects Christ. God loves us and wants us in His presence so much that He is extremely patient with us and gives us EVERY opportunity to choose Him. No, He cannot be in the presence of sin and does not condone it, but He is forgiving, long-suffering and patient, giving us every opportunity to choose to do what's pleasing in His sight.

I reminded my son to read his bible (so he would know for himself what God has said), be AWARE of the enemy's tricks and realize God NEVER stops loving you. God has designed us to win in life, no matter what the circumstance, but you must choose to prioritize God over everything.

Maybe you're caught in a habit or in a relationship that you know doesn't honor God. Maybe you feel as though you can't talk to God or you feel like He doesn't hear your prayers. Remind yourself that feelings change, but God doesn't. He has given us His modus operandi in His Word, the Bible. He genuinely wants YOU in His presence, to love on YOU...forever. Don't treasure the habit, the pattern of behavior or inappropriate relationship more than you cherish God. Give Him priority; talk to Him. Go ahead... He's listening.

Notes

Meditate

If we confess our sins, He is faithful and just to forgive us our sins and to cleanse us from all unrighteousness.

1 John 1:9, ESV

For, "everyone who calls on the name of the Lord will be saved."

Romans 10:13, NIV

Who wants all people to be saved and to come to the knowledge of the truth.

1 Timothy 2:4, NIV

---

she said, "No one, Lord." And Jesus said to her, "neither do I condemn you; go and sin no more."

John 8:11, NKJV

Prayer

God, Your Word says that if I confess with my mouth and believe in my heart that You raised Jesus from the dead that I would be saved. I believe that You are God and Jesus is Your Son Whom You raised from the dead; therefore, I am saved. Father, since it is Your heart that all men be saved, I take it upon myself to plant the seed in the hearts of all those I meet, including my family and friends. God, I thank You for watering the seed and allowing me to work alongside You in reaching the lost. I claim my family, friends, and coworkers for Your kingdom, Lord. Grant me the strength to resist temptation, remind me of my authority to rebuke the enemy and teach me Your Word so that I won't sin against You, in Jesus' name, amen.

Confession

I receive strength from the Lord to resist the devil and flee from temptation. I am saved despite how I may feel or mistakes I may make. If I fall into sin, God is faithful and just to forgive me once I confess and washes me clean as if it never happened. I am righteous because He made me so, therefore, I have a right to be in His presence. I declare that I listen to the Father and the voice of the enemy, I choose not to follow. God loves me and has set me up to win every time in every situation for His glory and honor.

Day 30: God & The College Life

On your graduation day, you may feel a little anxious about your future. I'm here to tell you that it is bright when you have Christ as your anchor. Christ is your anchor when you rely on Him for everything. Hopefully, you have been relying on God all your life, and it's not a big deal. For those of you who are new to this, or you've relied on your parents' relationship with Christ, you need to use the summer before leaving for the campus to start!

College is an exciting adventure! You will LEARN so much and make lots of great memories as well as mistakes. This is a time where you stand on your own two feet and get your first taste of being an adult, learning what it's like to run your own household. It can be daunting or refreshing depending on where your relationship is with Christ.

There have been teens, actively involved in their church youth group, Christian camps and never missed a Sunday worship service, who fell off the wagon after a semester in college. They were beaten down by their peers teasing them for studying the Bible, time constraints due to schoolwork and extracurricular activities or work, or by agnostic professors who taught their classes with disdain for God.

There will be instances in college where YOU will come up against the things I just mentioned, and more, but YOU must be anchored in Christ to be successful. When you rely on Christ, He can instruct you on how to respond to those who ridicule you for spending time with Him. Then you will be able to practice what you preach while patiently waiting for the door to be opened to lead some of those same naysayers to Christ.

When my eldest son went off to college, he was assured of his salvation. There are a lot of things going on in the world, and you will encounter them in school. In my house, the rule is if you live here, you go to church. When he relocated to Arizona, he stopped attending church. Without his pipeline to The Source, it was easy for him to forgo praying and spending time with God.

The good news is, you can ALWAYS start again! God is patient and is rooting for your success. When you are ready to talk to Him, He is very eager to listen and respond. Relying on God may seem hard at first, but when you do, it produces such peace in life. You can depend on God for any and everything: study help, relationship advice, help with your finances, healing, comfort during a loss, friendship, wisdom...whatever you need.

Your college experience will be based on what you believe, speak and do DAILY. It can be an incredible journey of self-discovery and revelation OR a chore to be dreaded; it's all based on YOU and the foundation you choose to stand on. When you are embarking on your journey of becoming an adult, be sure to INVITE God into your daily routine, continuously learning from His firm foundation — His Word. When you do this, He makes your way prosperous, places your mind in His perfect peace, and grants you precisely what you confessed.

Notes

Meditate

Truly, I say to you, whoever says to this mountain, 'Be taken up and thrown into the sea,' and does not doubt in his heart, but believes that what he says will come to pass, it will be done for him. Therefore I tell you, whatever you ask in prayer, believe that you have received it, and it will be yours.
Mark 11:23-24, ESV

Beloved, I pray that all may go well with you and that you may be in good health, as it goes well with your soul.
3 John 2, ESV

This Book of the Law shall not depart from your mouth, but you shall meditate on it day and night, so that you may be careful to do according to all that is written in it. For then you will make your way prosperous, and then you will have good success.
Joshua 1:8, ESV

You keep him in perfect peace whose mind is stayed on you, because he trusts in You.

Isaiah 26:3, ESV

Prayer

Father, You said that if I meditate on Your words and speak them in faith, that I would have what I say and that I will have good success. I believe You and expect Your wisdom to guide me in making the right decisions daily so that I may honor You. Lord, set my schedule and help me develop a habit of renewing my mind and thoughts with Your Word. I declare it is well with my soul and that I walk in divine health. As I meditate on the scriptures, You make my way prosperous, fill me with peace and equip me to remove the obstacles in my life. I thank You for the victory in advance and ask Holy Spirit to keep Your truths at the forefront of my mind, in Jesus' name, amen.

Confession

I declare that my ways are successful; everything I touch prospers. I do what is pleasing to my Father. Thus, He makes even my enemies be at peace with me. I say what God says; I agree with His Word. My mind stays on the Father, and He supplies wisdom. I have all that I need in Him. I can do all things through Christ.

Day 31: Chores & Your Reasonable Service

When I come home, I want to relax and enjoy my family. That is hard to do when everything is out of its place. When you share space with other people, you should be considerate and respectful; sharing the responsibilities of maintaining an enjoyable atmosphere. It is a soothing experience to relax in a tidy home. The atmosphere of the house is affected by the level of cleanliness; I think that's why I love the Girl Scout saying, "leave a place cleaner than you found it."

Leaving a place CLEANER than you found it can be done in several ways, usually with chores and reasonable basic service. Sometimes people say the two interchangeably, but they are two different things. Chores are what you contribute to the household because you are part of the family. Reasonable service is whatever is deemed sensible for the situation. It is your reasonable service if it is needed, fair, necessary or you're responsible for it. For example, cleaning your room is your reasonable service but mopping the kitchen floor is a chore assigned to help maintain the overall appearance and atmosphere of the house.

When I was a young child living at home with my parents, I had chores. My routine was homework, chores then free time. Nowadays, my family is almost always out and about checking off items on our busy schedule. As we've gotten busier, I've significantly relaxed the emphasis on chores and almost wholly dismissed reasonable service to our detriment. Consequently, the kids remark that I am more pleasant when outside of our home.

Our house is NOT the place where the kids hang out. In fact, we rarely have company because eight times out of ten, we did not clean up after our frantic "getting ready" routine before leaving the house. Because we don't have a "place for every object," it can get messy. Our attitude, mental clarity, and our mood gets "messy" as well. It's difficult to be patient and accommodating when your attitude has been negatively affected by a messy environment.

When your space is a MESS not only will your attitude be sour, your ability to focus in such an overwhelmingly messy environment slows the learning process. You could probably be more productive if you cleaned up! Clutter plays a significant role in how you feel about yourself as well. Messy spaces not only make you feel embarrassed and overwhelmed but cause anxiety and stress too. Dirty rooms cost you too much. Mess and clutter cost your focus, feelings of well-being, creativity and time. Keep negative feelings away and boost your mood by taking the time to clean up and organize.

Organizing is not one of my strengths, and I'm not fond of cleaning up, but I'm working on changing that. I've saved this devotion for last so that you know there will always be things you will be working out. I want you to know that you will still be a student of life, changing things about yourself and keeping up with the changes around you. It is a process, a journey, which we are all on. Each route is slightly different, but we all must walk it out. I want to STRESS that the mission is much better, goes smoother and ends successfully when you have Jesus Christ. He is the one who gives you the power to stand firm on His Word to accomplish the goals in your life. That is why giving Him your time is so beneficial. It is only in Him do you have a 100% guarantee of finishing the journey as a winner, successfully attaining all you desired and even being content with the things that perhaps slipped away. It isn't a chore to serve Him. It's an honor AND your reasonable service.

Notes

Meditate

I am not saying this because I am in need, for I have learned to be content whatever the circumstances.
Philippians 4:11, NIV

Now it is God who makes both us and you stand firm in Christ...
2 Corinthians 1:21, NIV

He replied, "Blessed rather are those who hear the word of God and obey it."
Luke 11:28, NIV

Now that you know these things, you will be blessed if you do them.
John 13:17, NIV

Prayer

Father, in the name of Jesus, I call those things that be not as though they were, according to Your word in Romans 4:17. I declare that I master organizing and cleaning. I ask for Your help in garnering strength and desire needed to maintain the cleanliness and order of my home. Lord, I pray that You prompt my family/roommates to clean up after themselves and be active in helping to maintain the order & cleanliness of our space. Holy Spirit, help me realize that cleaning my home and serving my family is serving Jesus; my divinely appointed way of honoring God's word. Lord, remind me to carve out time to clean my home. May I put my hands to cleaning and see it prosper, in Jesus' name, amen.

Confession

I make it my ambition to never tire of keeping a clean home, and I do so without complaining. My family/roommates see my efforts & choose to keep their area clean as well. I watch over my household affairs; I am not idle (Proverbs 3:27). I effectively manage my home, giving no room for enemy slander (1 Timothy 5:14). I declare I manage my household well according to God's word (1 Timothy 3:12). I do not get weary cleaning house and organizing my things because I receive the desired results; I reap what I sow. I put my hands to cleaning, and it prospers. I will not give up, and I declare that I see results. It is so, in Jesus' name.

Salvation

If you don't know Jesus as your personal Lord & Savior {you don't have a personal relationship with God), I'd love the opportunity to introduce you.

God loves YOU and wants YOU to choose to be with Him. He has provided all YOU need to experience abundant life. (John 3:16; John 10:10) We are born into sin because of Adam's disobedience but God sent Jesus to reconcile us to Him! (Romans 3:23; Romans 6:23; Romans 5:19) Jesus died in our place so WE could be alive to God! (Romans 5:8; 1 Corinthians 15:3-4)

God is waiting for you to reach out to Him in prayer to receive His FREE gift of new life. All you have to do is BELIEVE what His Word says. If you DO believe and you want to become His child, say this prayer out loud from your heart:

God, You said that if I declare with my mouth, "Jesus is Lord," and believe in my heart that You raised Jesus from the dead, then I will be saved. I declare that with my heart I believe and am justified, and it is with my mouth that I profess my faith and am saved. Thank You for forgiving me of my sins, washing me clean as if I never sinned and making me righteous! I receive Your gift of salvation! In Jesus' name, amen.

If you prayed that prayer, you are now a child of God – welcome to the Family of God! Email me at faithslinger@hotmail.com to let me know that you've made the BEST decision of your life.

About The Author

Tenisha N. Collins is an accountant, editor, entrepreneur and author who is working towards becoming a full time Christian marriage counselor. She is the daughter of Raymond & Felecia Johnson of Louisville, Kentucky and has one brother and five sisters.

A graduate of the University of Kentucky's Gatton College of Business, she holds a Bachelor's of Science in Accounting. When Tenisha's not preparing corporate and individual income taxes at the firm where she works part time, she is balancing her mom life (driving teens to volleyball tournaments, football games, show choir rehearsals, violin recitals, Girl Scout cookie booths, tutoring sessions, play dates, and PTSA/student government meetings) with her wife and entrepreneur life (Collins, Ink. Editing & Proofreading Services, Brand Ambassador for It Works! Global, and Strong Marriage Christian Counseling).

Tenisha is the founder of Strong Marriage, a Facebook group with the aim of equipping spouses with the tools necessary to love each other like Christ loves the church. She is also the Los Angeles Social Media Team Leader and Contract Editor for Wife Talk, Inc.

She loves God and desires that everyone who reads her books would love Him too. White cake, Batman, Hulk, Black Panther, Wonder Woman, cheese pizza, bread, shrimp, royal blue, taking family photos, and the beach are some of her favorite things. However, Tenisha is MOST delighted by her highest calling – daughter of the Most High God (26 years), wife to Chris (25 years) and mom of Chris II, Daniel, Faith and Joy.

Made in the USA
San Bernardino, CA
10 May 2018